Sustainability Leader in a Green Business Era

Sustainability Leader in a Green Business Era

A Middle East Perspective

Amr Sukkar, PhD

BEP BUSINESS EXPERT PRESS

First published in 2020 by
Business Expert Press, LLC
222 East 46th Street, New York, NY 10017
www.businessexpertpress.com

ISBN-13: 978-1-95152-785-3 (paperback)
ISBN-13: 978-1-95152-786-0 (e-book)

Business Expert Press Environmental and Social Sustainability for Business Advantage Collection

Collection ISSN: 2327-333X (print)
Collection ISSN: 2327-3348 (electronic)

First edition: 2020

10 9 8 7 6 5 4 3 2 1

Printed in the United States of America.

Abstract

The SME sector in the Middle East has always been one of the main drivers of the economy, but this sector rarely showed an interest in PPP ("'People, Planet, and Profits'"), the environment, and sustainability. From interviews with SME leaders the author suggests a widespread lack of conviction of the importance of the environment, and insistence that short-term profitability is the main focus. However, things are changing now and there is more pressure on businesses to take an interest in these issues; yet, there is a lack of clarity about the attributes (characteristics, personality, competencies, qualities, or character) of leaders who can run an SME and who have a predisposition to focus on environmental and resource sustainability.

Keywords

Leadership; SMEs; sustainable development; environment; sustainability leader; SME leaders

Contents

Preface

Before the Revolution, Egypt suffered considerable neglect of environmental issues. Heavily subsidized fuel was used at an alarming rate, causing considerable damage to the atmosphere. Restraints on fuel subsidies currently being implemented by the new administration in Egypt have meant a new emphasis on the efficient use of resources. With the slow rebuilding of the economy in Egypt and the government's efforts to promote tourism again, attention is being placed on the environment which had been neglected for a long time. Additionally, Egypt faces problems regarding electricity and water supply.

As this book was completed, the new Egyptian president, Abdelfattah El-Sisi, attended the United Nations Climate Summit on September 23, 2014, in New York to discuss climate change problems and the consequences on peoples' lives. In reviewing the national effort to deal with climate change and its negative effects on Egypt, he invited the developed countries to invest in renewable energy projects in the Middle East to help with the shift to a more environmental-friendly business model in the region. He said

> Our nations suffer from aggravated energy crises at a time when they look to achieve high rates of growth, which requires an expansion of renewable energy projects to provide energy with the transformation to an economic model that is more environmentally friendly.

He added, "I invite developed countries, financial institutions and the private sector to invest in these projects." This was intended to motivate public and private sector organizations to adopt the sustainability concept in their daily work activities, and the idea has been received positively. For example, after the recent directives of President Sisi for the necessity to rationalize energy consumption, Mr. Alaptati Majdi, governor of Beni Suef (one of the governorates of Egypt), issued a decision to rationalize the consumption of electricity in the offices of the governorate and placed advertisements on the streets. This decision was aimed to decrease the current consumption by 50 percent and included promoting the use of solar energy in lighting advertisements to help toward paying the cost.

There is widespread concern from environmental experts that the way many companies in Egypt are operating might compromise future generations in terms of the availability of resources. Interest in "People, Planet, and Profits" (PPP) was sometimes espoused by multinationals operating in Egypt in the past, but some of these companies have left the country with the Revolution and economic dislocation, although they represented only a part of the economy. The SME sector in Egypt has always been one of the main drivers of the economy, but this sector rarely showed an interest in PPP, the environment, and sustainability. Anecdotal evidence from interviews with SME leaders by the author suggests a widespread lack of conviction in the importance of the environment, and insistence that short-term profitability is the focus. However, things are changing now and there is more pressure on businesses to take an interest in these issues. Yet, there is a lack of clarity about the attributes (characteristics, personality, competencies, qualities, or character) of leaders who can run an SME and who have a predisposition to focus on environmental and resource sustainability.

The above illustrates why the author tackled this subject in this book.

Amr Sukkar

Acknowledgments

I would like to thank the people who helped and supported me until I finished this work. I wish to specially thank my family; my mother, and my wife for their ongoing support and understanding and my father **Mr. Essam Sukkar,** for keeping me motivated throughout all my life projects with his inspirational and encouraging guidance.

Definition of Terms

A Change Agent: "Is any individual or group that initiates and/ or facilitates change" (Duncan 1978, p. 1022).

Attributes: Characteristics, character or personality, competence, qualities, attitudes, beliefs, convictions, and values.

Environmental Champion: "Someone who can attractively express a personal vision about environmental protection that is in tune with both industry's needs and wider public concern." (Menon and Menon 1997, p. 61).

Environmental Sustainability: "The use of business practices to reduce a company's impact on the natural, physical environment" (Wheelen and Hunger 2011, p. 56).

Leadership Style: "Refers to how an individual gathers input, presents ideas, and mobilizes people, whether they are employees, suppliers, customers, or the community" (Dutra, Everaert, Fust, and Millen 2011, p. 2).

Leadership: "A process of influence that occurs within the context of relationships between leaders and their collaborators that involves: establishing direction (shared vision); aligning resources; and generating motivation and providing inspiration." (Taylor 2011, p. 5).

Life Cycle Assessment (LCA): "Is a tool for the systematic evaluation of the environmental aspects of a product or service system through all stages of its life cycle. LCA provides an adequate instrument for environmental decision support. Reliable LCA performance is crucial to achieve a life-cycle economy." (United Nations Environment Program; p. 1).

Management: "Refers to the set of activities, and often the group of people, involved in four general functions, including planning, organizing, leading and coordinating activities." (Note that the four functions recur throughout the organization and are highly integrated.). (McNamara 1997).

Organization, Firm, Company, and Corporation: These terms are used in this study to mean a company.

Organizational Culture: "Pattern of shared basic assumptions that the group learned as it solved its problems of external adaptation and internal integration, which has worked well enough to be considered valid and, therefore, to be taught to new members as the correct way you perceive, think, and feel in relation to those problems" (Schein 1993, p. 20).

SMEs (The Small and Medium Enterprises): The definition of SMEs is different from one country to another and according to Yu and Bell (2007) "there is no universally accepted definition of a SME" (p. 20).

Social Responsibility: "Proposes that a private corporation has responsibilities to society that extend beyond making a profit" (Wheelen and Hunger 2011, p. 120).

Sustainability Leader: "Someone who inspires and supports action towards a better world" (Visser and Courtice 2011, p. 2).

In this research particularly, the sustainability leader is a person who focuses on the environmental aspects of sustainability and can lead his company to achieve its objectives with security for the environment or cares about avoiding damage to the surrounding environment. "Leader" in this study refers to top management, represented by a Company Owner, President in charge or CEO and does not, for the sake of this research, include leaders in general terms.

Sustainability Performance: "Can be defined as the performance of a company in all dimensions and for all drivers of corporate sustainability" (Schaltegger and Wagner 2006, p. 2).

Sustainability: "Organizational approaches aimed at achieving a balance be- tween short-term organizational goals and long-term enterprise and social responsibility" (Pearce, Manz, and Akanno 2013, p. 248).

Sustainable Development: "Development which takes care of not only the present but also future generations to meet their needs" (Godfrey and Manikas 2012, p. 1).

Sustainable Future: "Is the idea that sits business system which sustains natural and human resources" (Andreas et al. 2011, p. 3).

Sustainable system: Is one that "fulfills present and future needs while using, and not harming, renewable resources and unique human environmental resources of a site: air, land, water, energy, mineral resources, and human ecology and/or those of other (off-site) sustainable systems" (Andreas et al. 2011, p. 3).

Dr. Amr Sukkar

CHAPTER 1

Introduction

Chapter Objectives

- Understand the business sustainability concept.
- Impart basic knowledge about the UN SDGS.
- Create awareness about the sustainable development challenges in Egypt.

Overview of the Origin of Sustainable Development Concept

Overpopulation and globalization of markets have added to domestic pressures from overexploitation of resources all over the world. The relevancy of the environmental sustainability concept has increased in many countries as there is more awareness and understanding of the impact of environmental issues on society and economic growth. Research on the natural environment and its relation to business has developed considerably over the years. Many countries in the Asia-Pacific region and the United States are expecting economic, social, and environmental factors to convince the manufacturing companies to consider sustainability more seriously. Nowadays, corporate sustainability is an important topic for both academic research and businesses.

Overview of "sustainable development": the term "sustainable development" was first made popular by the WCEB, also known as the World Commission on Economic Development. The WCEB defined sustainable development as "development action targeted for meeting the needs of the present without hindering future generations from fulfilling their own needs." The WCEB stated that in order to realize sustainable development, the adoption of environmental, economic, and equity principles is necessary. Such a statement was, then, highly questioned due to the old prejudice that caring for the environment and establishing social equity go against making money. Over time, corporations began to show commitment to achieving sustainable development. With regard to principles of sustainable development, Elkington (1998) stated that sustainable development can only be achieved by applying three basic principles which are environmental integrity, economic prosperity, and social equity.

Environmental integrity: The environmental integrity principle guarantees that the ecosystem, that is, land, air, and water, is not harmed by any human activities. It is perceived that the ecosystem has a very limited regenerative ability; therefore, human-related events such as population growth and pollution compromise the integrity of the environment. Thus, if the natural environment is, by any means, threatened or compromised then the basic resources necessary for human life, such as food and water, will be threatened as well.

Social equity: The social equity principle guarantees that all members in a society have equal opportunities and equal access to resources. The WCED document released in 1987 stated that sustainability is a universal goal implying that all members of future generations, members of developing and developed countries alike, have the right to equal access to resources.

Economic prosperity: The economic prosperity principle endorses an adequate quality of life through organizations and individual members in society. Economic prosperity calls for the creation and distribution of goods that will most likely elevate the quality of life around the world in addition to the establishment of open and competitive markets that endorse efficiency, wealth creation, and innovation. It was found that economic prosperity is heavily linked to social equity and environmental integrity. For instance, to meet basic needs such as food and shelter, people tend to compromise the long-term health of the natural environment in the process. It is estimated that millions of hectares of forest areas are annihilated annually for the production of fuels, wood, and fertile land for agriculture. Therefore, it is perceived that a society that fails to realize economic prosperity will eventually compromise the health and well-being of its individuals.

Corporate sustainable development: Business is the production of goods or services for the customers in exchange for other services, goods, or money. Particular organizations and the market sector can be referred to as businesses. When many persons are working in one company, they are making business to produce a specific service or good in a good manner in order to raise their company in the market to reach for the lead and to be one of the most important companies in its field.

Sustainable development is a new way for people to use resources before they run out; in other words it is the development that meets the needs of the present without compromising the ability of future generations to meet their own needs. For the business community, sustainable development is extremely important and more than just window-dressing, as the companies can compete by adopting sustainable practices in order to increase both shareholder value and their markets. The company's value differentiates it from its competitors as the products and services that yield tangible results for the company's target customers. There are two important parts of a business model, which are production and marketing. The production side combines many factors including activities and mechanisms for providing goods and services. On the other hand, the marketing side combines those mechanisms in order to sell the products, whether they are goods or services. The latter is also known as capturing value but the first is known as creating value. The economic, social, and environmental benefits can be delivered by the business model for sustainable development.

The success of the business models for sustainable development can be determined by disparate factors; trade-offs among different sustainable development goals (economic, social, environmental) need to be recognized and addressed, and the ongoing monitoring and evaluation need to be built into business model. The idea of sustainable development has become a way of creating affirmation, yet it is not the first thought for some business executives. For most, the thought stays hypothetical and theoretical. Guaranteeing an affiliation's capital base is a recognized business rule. The associations are unable to perceive the likelihood of extension of this idea to the world norm and HR. If sensible progression is to fulfill its potential, it must be fused into the masterminding and estimation systems of business endeavors. For that to happen, the thought must be verbalized in words which are common to business pioneers.

The business response was the idea of eco-effectiveness, uniting ecological and financial execution to make more regard for business itself as well as for the whole gathering, fundamentally, with less impact. Numerous organizations are today close to the cutting edge toward eco-capability, and it has in like manner transformed into a comprehensively recognized methodology supported by the European Commission. Clearly, more businesses need to get eco-capability, not only the multinationals arranged in the industrialized countries, but the small and medium endeavors in all sectors in all countries. Sustainable advancement is based on three factors: financial development, natural parity, and social advancement. These things have dependably been part of the motivation for maintainability; however, the social factor has received less consideration. That is changing; far more noteworthy attention is being set now on social advancement, particularly on what business is doing. This has opened up a number of issues. For a firm to achieve sustainable development it must first fulfill all three basic principles.

Environmental integrity may be achieved through corporate environmental management. Corporate environmental management is an approach made by a firm to reduce its ecological footprint that is the impact of its production processes on the environment, such as waste and carbon emissions. Such management can be achieved by pollution control and product stewardship. Pollution control refers to the proper disposal of wastes by a company, while product stewardship refers to using fewer materials for product design and proper recycling and reuse of products at the end of their life. Companies may seek social equity through corporate social responsibility. Corporate social responsibility encompasses three processes: environmental assessment, stake-holder management, and social issues management. Environmental assessment involves the identification of social, economic, and environmental issues and responding to them accordingly. Stakeholder management involves responding to individuals outside organizations as well as responding to the natural environment (Starik 1995). On the other hand, social management refers to tackling social issues, for instance, the decision not to employ children as labor.

Economic prosperity can be achieved through value creation. A firm can create value via their own products and goods. It can create value through the production of novel and different products desired by consumers, thereby elevating the effectiveness of its products which can be achieved by decreasing input costs or achieving production efficiencies. A firm can capture the value it creates by selling its goods or services at prices that exceed their costs. To conclude, the road to implementing a sustainable development philosophy will be different for smaller businesses, but with ingenuity, perseverance, and cooperation, they can achieve the desired result. In the end it is apparent that corporate prosperity is dependent upon how successful an organization is at achieving sustainable development. In addition to achieving corporate welfare, sustainable development also constitutes an ethical duty that must be exerted by the present generations for the well-being of future generations. There are hundreds of definitions of sustainability. According to Andreas and Cooperman, a well-known definition of the term sustainability related to business or development is the one coined by Gro Harlem, former prime minister of Norway and chairperson of the Brundtland Commission. The concept of sustainability is included as a requirement to "meet the needs of the present without compromising the ability of future generations to meet their needs" (Andreas et al. 2011, p. xii). More recently, researchers have proposed that we should focus more on interdependencies between business and society and take collaborative approaches to create system change (Baas 2008; Porter 2006; Boons and Roome 2005; Svendsen and Laberge 2005; in Loorbach, van Bakel, Whiteman, and Rotmans 2010). This change will cause SMEs to move from being careless of environmental concerns in their business plans and actions, to measuring their environmentally related performance, for example, in terms of waste production or resource use, adoption of ISO 14001, or how regulation influences performance. Moreover, some researchers have labeled as "enviropreneurship" the efforts made by individuals to bring ideas and motivations to increase the ecological sustainability concept of their organization.

For many years, CEOs of both major companies and international organizations such as the United Nations have talked about, or even put on a pedestal, the topic of sustainability as an inevitable challenge to change, as well as an imperative to change.

The UN SDGs (Sustainable Development Goals) as a Broad Universal Context for Sustainability

According to UN Environment Management group, the sustainable development goals (SDGs, also referred to the global goals) are the blueprint to achieve a better and more sustainable future for all. The key element of 2030 Agenda, they address the global challenges we face, including those related to poverty, inequality, climate, environmental degradation, prosperity, and peace and justice. The goals interconnect and, in order to ensure a just transition that leaves no one behind, it is important that we achieve each goal and target by 2030. Each SDG is comprised of a set of subtargets. Additionally, each goal has a set of indicators, jointly known as the global indicator framework, with which to assess progress. The global indicator framework was developed by the Inter-Agency and Expert Group on SDG Indicators (IAEG-SDGs) and agreed to as a practical starting point at the 47th session of the UN Statistical Commission held in March 2016. The report of the commission, which included the global indicator framework, was then taken note of by ECOSOC at its 70th session in June 2016. The links in the list of SDGs in Figure 1.1 will take you to the goals' unique targets and indicators, as well as recent updates on progress.

Figure 1.1 *The sustainable development goals*

Source: https://unemg.org/our-work/supporting-the-sdgs/the-un-sustainable-development-goals/

The Sustainable Development Goals

1. No poverty—end poverty, in all its forms, everywhere.
2. Zero hunger—end hunger, achieve food security and improved nutrition, and improve agriculture.
3. Good health and well-being—ensure healthy lives and promote well-being for all, at all ages.
4. Quality educations—ensure inclusive and equitable quality education and promote lifelong learning opportunities for all.
5. Gender equality—achieve gender equality and empower all women and girls.
6. Clean water and sanitation—ensure sustainable management and availability of water and sanitation for all.
7. Affordable energy—ensure access to affordable, reliable, sustainable, and modern energy for all.
8. Decent work and economic growth—promote sustained, inclusive, and sustainable economic growth, full and productive employment, and decent work for all.
9. Industry innovation and infrastructure—build resilient infrastructure, promote inclusive and sustainable industrializations, and foster innovation.
10. Reduced inequalities—reduce inequality within and among countries.
11. Sustainable cities and communities—make cities and human settlements inclusive, safe, resilient, and sustainable.
12. Responsible consumption and production—ensure sustainable consumption and production patterns.
13. Climate action—take urgent action to combat climate change and its impacts.
14. Life below water—conserve and sustainably use the oceans, seas, and marine resources for sustainable development.
15. Life on land—protect, restore, and promote sustainable use of terrestrial ecosystems, sustainably manage forests, combat desertification, halt and reverse land degradation, and halt biodiversity loss.
16. Peace, justice, and strong institutions—promote peaceful and inclusive societies for sustainable development, provide access to justice for all, and build effective, accountable institutions at all levels.

17. Partnerships for the goals—strengthen the means of implementation and revitalize the global partnership for sustainable development.

Overview of Sustainability Development Challenge in Egypt

According to the official *State Information Service* in Egypt (2014), "Egypt currently faces several environmental challenges, which place the prospects of future generations in jeopardy and lead to the depletion of natural resources" (State Information Service, para. 1). Accordingly, the Egyptian Environmental Affairs Agency, in its efforts to achieve sustainable development, attempts to address these challenges by maintaining and managing natural resources within the framework of sustainable development. However, it can be suggested that little progress can be made until organizations in Egypt become interested in these concerns. For the organizations to become interested in environmental challenges there must be some involvement from the leaders.

The problems related to natural environmental resources which play an important role to support the business sector are several. At the top of the list are water shortage, energy shortfalls, the relative nonimplementation of laws to protect the environment, and the declining levels of awareness of environmental issues. For example, the River Nile is the lifeline of Egypt as it services industrial and agricultural demand. Nowadays, Egypt is facing an annual water deficit of around seven billion cubic meters. In fact, the United Nations is already alerting conservationists that Egypt could run out of water by the year 2025. Moreover, Ethiopia started working on building El Nahda dam on the River Nile. The project has raised concerns in Cairo about its potential impact on Egypt's annual share of water. Another important issue is that Egypt faces chronic gasoline shortages and frequent power cuts, which negatively affect the business sector and which have begun to put some pressure on businesses to be more concerned about the environmental resources, as Mr. Salah Abo Yazid, financial advisor to the Holding Company for Chemical Industries in Egypt, emphasized.

Production rates for nitrogen fertilizers, which rely on natural gas, declined during the year 2014 by up to 40 percent, and this is having a negative impact on the productivity of companies and their subsidiaries. These have been affected significantly by the energy crisis in Egypt during the last period, particularly the National Cement Company which decreased its production capacity by 50 percent, due to lower rates of gas supplied. According to the U.S. Energy Information Administration (2014), Egypt is the largest oil and natural gas consumer in Africa, accounting for more than 20 percent of total oil consumption and more than 40 percent of total dry natural gas consumption in Africa in 2013.

From 2009 to 2013 much of the natural gas consumed in Egypt was used to fuel electric power plants. Since 2013 Egypt has been facing natural gas supply shortages and the natural gas production declined by an average of 3 percent annually; thus there are frequent power cuts. Gas, gasoline, coal, oil, and natural gas are fossil fuel resources and their consumption leads to global warming and climate change. Furthermore, fossil fuels are finite resources and they can irreparably harm the environment (Environmental and Energy Study Institution 2014). Figure 1.2

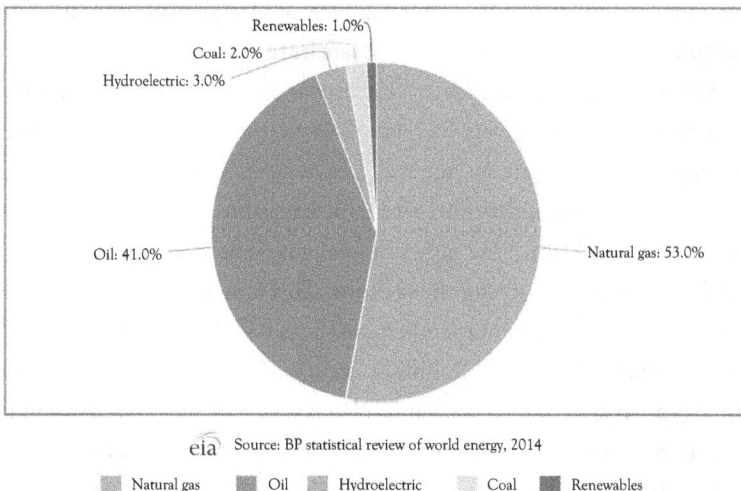

eia   Source: BP statistical review of world energy, 2014

Natural gas   Oil   Hydroelectric   Coal   Renewables

Figure 1.2 Energy consumption in Egypt

shows the high consumption of fossil fuels and how renewable energy in Egypt is not used.

The above statements highlight two important and noteworthy issues:

1. The presence of sustainability practices in different industries and companies in Egypt could have prevented such depletion of valuable resources as well as keeping productivity rates uninterrupted.
2. Leaders who apply and are aware of sustainability concepts and practices are crucial for the prevention or reduction of natural resources depletion. The need for such leaders is thus a pressing issue.

The need for such leaders in Egypt becomes even more pressing when we further notice the effect on water and air pollution that the misuse of such resources can have.

Egyptians obtain about 97 percent of their water from the Nile River and the rest from winter rain and nonrenewable groundwater aquifers. Much of this water is polluted through industrial activities. Since the 1950s, many industries have developed in Egypt along the Nile Delta producing industrial waste which is often discarded in the water creating a major chemical threat to agricultural land. Moreover, the industrial companies in Egypt are one of the main reasons for air pollution, due, for example, to the practice of open-air waste burning.

Several of the environmental problems in Egypt stem from the long-term provision of generous fuel subsidies by the government, in order to keep influential people (such as car owners) contented. According to Prime Minster Mahlab (2014), Egypt has some of the lowest energy prices in the world, and the cash-strapped government spends more than a fifth of its budget keeping them down. This is significantly more than both health and education spending combined, which take up 64 billion pounds ($8.9 billion) and 26 billion pounds ($3.6 billion), respectively. The Egyptian government announced that it would spend an additional 70 billion Egyptian pounds ($9.8 billion) on energy subsidies in the fiscal year ending June 30, 2014. All this has, however, changed. One of the plans of the government in the near future is to remove the energy subsidies. To manage all complexities that are required to implement environmental sustainability in an organization and to cope with more limited resources, there is a need for a leader with special competencies (Ghaem 2013).

The statements above suggest that Egypt needs sustainability leaders. Sustainability practices converge around three elements: securing the environment, economic growth, and social development. The Sustainability Leadership Institute (2011) suggests that sustainability leaders are "individuals who are compelled to make a difference by deepening their awareness of themselves in relation to the world around them. In doing so, they adopt new ways of seeing, thinking and interacting that result in innovative, sustainable solution" (The Sustainability Leadership Institute 2011; para. 4).

Another definition of a sustainability leader is that of Visser and Courtice 2011: "someone who inspires and supports action toward a better world" (p. 2).

From the above statements a sustainability leader can be defined as the leader who constantly targets developing the three aspects of sustainability: environmental, social, and economic. In this research the sustainability leader is understood to be the person who focuses on the environmental aspects of sustainability and who can lead his company to achieve its objectives of preserving the environment or taking precautions to avoid damaging the surrounding environment.

The author conducted interviews with several Egyptian leaders of SMEs in order to ask them about their care and interest about the environment and social responsibility, and if a greater concern for the environment would be useful for their business. Mr. A, sales director of N. Company, revealed that

> In our company we don't care about environment or social responsibilities, it's seen as over cost without profit return. Only sometimes we produce our products for well-known brands with high quality standards, sometimes we use the residuals and wastes from the raw material to produce the same products with low quality and sell them to other clients.

Eng. K, CEO of F. Company, suggested that "Of course it is very important, we already care about that concept and now we recycle all our products." By contrast, Mr. N, general sales and export manager of M. Company, admitted that "If we don't see any profit return, we will not care about that. Our main concern is innovation in our products to gain more profit and to compete in the market." Mr. O, CEO of S. Company, also agreed that "Although we know we have an environmental problem from our production waste, which is the rice straw, until now we haven't thought of treating this problem." Taking a different line, Eng. R, CEO of T. Company, explained that "We follow Life Cycle Assessment (LCA) as a tool for sustainability performance evaluation; LCA provides an adequate instrument for environmental decision support" and when asked what he meant by LCA he said "Environmental quality certificates like the ISO 14000."

Of the five interviewees, only one of the SME leaders had incorporated environmental sustainability practices in his company for the sake of sustainability, while another, who recycled his product line, further asserted that they are doing so only because it has a positive impact on their profits rather than being a sustainability practice. This translates to 20 percent of the total participants being aware of the importance of environmental sustainability in SMEs or its impact on the environment.

The above-mentioned discussions, in addition to the practical work experience of the author as well as findings from the literature review, point to an actual gap represented by a clearly observed negative attitude toward sustainability practices conceived by SMEs leaders as opposed to the actual importance of sustainability to their companies. For example, many SMEs leaders expect that adopting sustainability will increase the cost base for their companies financially, while they cannot expect any profit out of following environmentally sustainable measures. This is despite the widespread belief that consideration for the environment is now much more imperative. So it would seem that lack of appropriate attitudes, competencies, and behaviors on the part of leaders has been stopping the progress of SMEs in adopting policies and strategies that could improve their concern for the environment. There is no doubt among many environmental experts that improvement is needed, but the leaders concerned seem to lack interest and conviction. However, financially,

Environmental costs have increasingly been internalized in the business with such charges as water consumption and waste disposal. As these costs increase, the cost of business increases and in the ever more competitive market place these costs will either reduce the profit or sales or both of SME. (DeLeeuw and Genoff 2000)

Sustainability goals for businesses have been defined as meeting a "triple bottom line comprised of environmental stewardship, standards of human dignity, and financial profit" (p. 3). There is obviously a need for leaders with the ability to take a strategic view of their businesses, as continually internalizing increased costs will eventually drive them out of business.

This book aims to address questions concerned with developing an understanding of a leader's attributes such as his characteristics, character, personality, competence, and qualities, which affect business sustainability. Drawing from social learning theory, it has been suggested that individuals learn appropriate behavior by observing others' actions and their consequences. It has been proposed that significant players, namely leaders, may strongly influence followers. Scholars suggest that leaders influence follower behavior by modeling appropriate behavior. According to social learning theory and social cognitive theory, learning that occurs through direct experience may also occur vicariously through observation of others' behaviors and their consequences (Hind et al. 2009). All the points above suggest that leaders may play a potentially major role in the followers' behavior toward the business sustainability concept. Culturally, in Egypt, there is a strong tendency for leaders to be dominant in driving subordinate behavior and company strategy. Questioning subordinates and making observations is likely to confirm this, regardless of what the leader says.

There is an increasing agreement that businesses need to embrace environmental sustainability, while recent research on leading sustainable development in the management field still provides only limited guidance on how this should be done. Preliminary research carried out by the author in Egypt suggests that there are few role models to suggest a way forward. We know that many SME leaders in Egypt are doubtful about achieving a PPP balance; we do not know the attributes of those SME leaders who think it might be possible and who are trying to achieve it.

A survey of Australian SMEs showed, during the process of interviewing larger corporations, that the latter became more aware of environmental responsibility than SMEs. Moreover, they showed that SMEs were generally slow to introduce environmental management controls. A small number of Chinese small firms have adopted a formal management system with concern for the environment and attitudes to sustainability management but have not yet incorporated these concerns into their business strategy.

Some researchers argue that organizations require a paradigm shift to adopt more sustainable ways of thinking and behaving (Whittaker et al. 2009; Linnenluecke and Griffiths 2010). Moreover, Millar and Gitsham (2013) state that more research is needed in order to change attitudes and behaviors in the workplace to make companies more interested in environmental sustainability and allow companies to be responsible for their future in terms of resource consumption. A sustainable future is the idea that fits a business system which sustains natural and human resources—again, a form of PPP.

According to Taylor "we can study certain types of leaders in particular contexts" (2011, p. 44). This generates knowledge on:

- Attributes of individual leaders
- The nature of group-based leadership processes
- The contextual factors that help leaders to emerge and be effective
- Interplay of factors to enhance sustainability attitudes and behaviors of employees (sustainability awareness and citizenship)

In Egypt, the tendency in business (especially in SMEs) is not to have group-based leadership processes. It is seen as a high power-distant culture. Contextual factors helping leaders emerge can be different from those in western countries. Rather than a selection process based on objective factors considered by a board of directors, leaders of SMEs in Egypt might be entrepreneurs or might be chosen due to nepotism.

In Egypt, people tend to depend on advice and instructions from authority figures and are used to a high degree of power distance where power is distributed unequally. This implies that changes would stem from the higher levels of a company, that is, from its leaders. Leaders with a high awareness of PPP would make business and environmental sustainability a priority in the business sector. This would have a positive impact on society and economic growth. There are external factors over which the company has very limited control including, but not limited to, socioeconomic and geopolitical factors. They further assert that top business leaders are held to be in charge of managing the whole *sustainability system*, where some seem to master this challenge better than others. Perhaps they are just more interested and concerned, as well as being more able. Indeed, this latter point raises the question of whether there are specific leaders' requirements or competencies that can be identified and further developed for CEOs of SMEs who want to be in the forefront of sustainability efforts. This further suggests the need to discover such competencies and requirements represented by the leader's attributes as addressed by the research objectives.

According to Andreas et al. (2011) the definition of a sustainable economic system might be "one which fulfills present and future needs while using, and not harming, renewable resources and unique human environmental resources of a site: Air, land, water, energy, mineral resources, and human ecology and/or those of other (off-site) sustainable systems" (p. 3). The SME CEO needs to take this on board mentally and then has to go about implementing changes to make sure this is translated into the management style and system of the organization.

Conclusion

A big gap exists between the laws and regulations enacted by the Egyptian government and their actual adoption and implementation by companies working in Egypt. Even when such laws, regulations, and policies are forced as a requirement for such companies to be able to start working, many companies find ways not to execute and adopt them. The reasons for such large gap are beyond the scope of this research but the fact stands that this is a big reality in Egypt. An extremely relevant example is the case with taxation. Almost all business and their legal accountants found, and still find, ways to circumvent much taxation, which resulted in a loss of billions of Egyptian pounds. For decades this has been the case until, all of a sudden, the government adopted another strategy that depended on deeply understanding people in every business sector, addressing all the range from very small to very large enterprises, focusing on the message that the government clearly understands their concerns and how to unthreateningly approach them. This illustrates the significance of understanding people's characteristics, personalities, behavioral dimensions, and values to beget optimal results. Based on insights into business leaders and managers this campaign was a great success.

The above-mentioned case as well as the ongoing situation in Egypt encouraged the author to adopt the methodology in this research, to target personal factors rather than contextual factors. In Egypt, sustainability is still a subject that the government is just starting to approach. Moreover in Egypt, unlike in developed countries, public communities and business sectors are not giving enough attention to environmental issues because most are concentrating on profits and survival. For the government to be successful in enacting and implementing sustainability programs, which has long been a global concern, it needs to approach such communities and business sectors in a way similar to the taxation case, based on insightful and in-depth knowledge of leaders and senior managers. Another contribution would be advising the government and the business sector about which leaders' personalities or attributes would fit such requirements for them to be able to hire such leaders. Leader attributes are suggested to be a rich and relatively immature field of research concerning sustainability and thus still requires further qualitative inspection and insights since it is unlikely that leaders share one and the same set of basic skills or personality traits. Hogan et al. (1994) highlight that some situations call for specific leader attributes in terms of personality and style. In other words, some attributes are particularly needed in specific situations. Sustainability issues might be one of those situational contexts that call for further inspection about leaders' attributes, and supporting that line of thought is that different studies of qualitative nature came out with different attributes; the studies were conducted in different contexts in terms of industries and cultures. Additionally, SMEs (Perrini and Tencati 2007), the focus of this research, are more reliant on personal relationships between leaders, managers, and their subordinates in achieving their goals and enacting their strategies, emphasizing the role of leader attributes in moving the whole organization to whatever goals are set, highlighting the importance of such leaders being sustainability oriented to enact sustainability programs, which further requires inspection concerning leaders' attributes (personal characteristics, values, beliefs, convictions) that most fit such endeavors. Large companies, on the contrary, as highlighted by Perrini and Tencati (2007), depend mainly on the organizational system, policies, and models of application in enacting their operations and achieving their objectives and strategic intents. This does not emphasize reliance on leader attributes in larger organizations as is the case with smaller ones, which is again the focus of this research. Additionally, collectivistic cultures, where relations play a critical role, call for more emphasis on inspecting such attributes since such a dimension of the Egyptian culture lends more emphasis to the above argument about SMEs as highlighted by Perrini and Tencati (2007).

CHAPTER 2

The Sustainability Concept in Organization Context

Chapter Objectives

- Define sustainable development as a discipline.
- Explain the frame and basics of sustainable organization.

The concept of sustainable business is relatively new. In 1987, the Brundtland Commission coined the phrase *sustainable development*, defining it as a development that "meets the needs of the present without compromising the ability of future generations to meet their own need" (Goldemberg 2007, p. 808). This concept was highlighted during the 1992 United Nations Conference on Environment and Development in Rio de Janeiro. Since this summit, organizations worldwide have adopted practices for sustainable development, economies, and societies. These practices converge around a concern for the environment, economic growth, and development of the world's poor. Sustainability is gaining increasing importance in the organizational context (e.g., Gitsham et al. 2009; McWilliams and Siegel 2001; Matten and Moon 2005; Pava and Kruausz 1996; United Nations Global Compact and Accenture 2010). "We define sustainability as organizational approaches aimed at achieving a balance between short-term organizational goals and long-term enterprise and social responsibility" (Pearce et al. 2013).

The following sections aim to provide a better understanding of the sustainability concept in the organizational context, as well as the relationship between business and the environment in context of that concept. In addition, they attempt to highlight the issue and probable solutions concerning the disparity between business profitability and the existence of sustainability leader in the SME and the organizational financial results.

Companies that have not adopted a sustainability concept will most probably have a main goal of growing and sustaining profitability and depend solely on financial indicators in monitoring performance. Hence, it is obvious that the practices of such companies will need a paradigm shift in order to adopt sustainability strategies. In addition, reporting schemes that can capture the company's all-inclusive performance indicators become of great value for decision makers to better forecast its future performance based on that strategic shift.

Maximizing human welfare is only possible if there are structures that encourage development, innovation, conservation, and discovery of new resources, where growth and increasing wealth through these methods lead to improved social and environmental quality. This suggests that sustainability can be achieved in this new era of responsibility only if a company is meeting the challenge and does what is right for the environment and society.

Hardman (2010) carried out a two-year grounded theory study of 24 successful leaders of increasingly sustainable organizations in education, business, and community. He found that sound stakeholder management from a social performance perspective positively correlates with the corporation's financial performance. This suggests that applying sustainability in companies has become an important competitive edge, where economic, social, and environmental indicators are more frequently presented, generating useful management scenarios for anticipation of new risks and market opportunities. If large corporations ignore social and environmental aspects, they put their profit at risk. "European citizens support the government's coordinating, and regulating role to reconcile the economic, environmental, and social dimensions of sustainability" (Zubir and Habidin 2012, p. 131) and, therefore, sustainability has become a primary competitive factor for many manufacturing companies in Europe. Moreover, Dutra et al. (2011) state that "sustainability is often linked to innovation management as an approach to creating competitive advantage or delivering long-term shareholder value" (p. 1). Following that line of thought, global sustainability challenges and economic opportunities may be presented to their companies. However, to capture such opportunities and gains a company needs to be able to manage aspects related to sustainability or, for that cause, be able to control it, which arouses concerns about how performance related to sustainability can be measured.

Conclusion

A sustainable organization or in another word business sustainability is a concept that suggests that it is the responsibility of the organizations and corporations operating within society to contribute toward economic, social, and environmental development that creates a positive impact on society at large. Although there is no fixed definition, the concept revolves around the fact that corporations need to focus beyond earning just profits. The inclusion of business sustainability is an attempt by the government to engage the businesses with the national development agenda. This calls for tools enabling sustainability activities within the organizations.

CHAPTER 3

Tools and Standards Enabling Sustainability

Chapter Objectives

- Understand the theoretical foundations and the importance of sustainability performance measurement.
- Explain simple and practical methods of sustainability performance evaluation.
- Provide alternative policy responses focusing on contemporary business sustainability.

Sustainability Performance Measurement

Sustainable practices need to be accountable and, thus, should be measurable as mentioned earlier. As companies implement sustainable programs by applying new policies or adopting new technologies, realistic and clear goals and objectives should be put forth and compared to actual performance on a systematic and continuous basis. Sustainable development requires methods and tools to measure and compare the environmental impact of human activities for the provision of goods and services. In this section the author will show the importance of sustainability performance evaluation and the most common indicators that are used to evaluate the companies' sustainability performance.

In an organization, on both subcultural and individual levels, addressing change in the context of sustainability goals may provide further insight into how sustainability develops within the organization.

Whittaker et al. (2009) suggest that sustainability-seeking organizations must make fundamental paradigm shifts away from their current linear, cradle-to-grave operational models toward a more integrative, eco-effective model. Researchers have also identified different methods to operationalize sustainability within organizations. As Bakel, Loorbach, and Whiteman (2007) remark, the studies in this field can measure environmental performances of organizations, for example, the adoption of ISO 14001 regulations and their influence on performance, resource use, and waste production. Thus, it is evident that sustainability implementation methods and standards are well defined and structured for the interested parties in adopting this concept.

Fiksel et al. (1999) argue that "sustainability performance measurement (SPM) must be approached as a systematic business process in order to be integrated effectively into company strategic planning and day-to-day operations" (p. 2). Sustainability performance can be defined as a company performance in all dimensions and for all drivers of organization sustainability (Schaltegger and Wagner 2006). The concept of multidimensional performance evaluation is based on the triple bottom line theory. Triple bottom line entails the comprehensive management reporting of business results and development of the economic entity with a balance of environmental, social, and economic capital (Lorenzoni et al. 2000). To identify such balance, it is essential to explore how company products or practices impact the environment and society. According to Epstein and Roy (2001) we can measure the sustainability actions and performance by:

- Weight given to environmental R&D budgets
- Expenditure on environment-conscious technology
- Expenditure on societal initiatives
- Weight given to prevention/safety programs
- Weight given to ISO certifications
- Procedures to reduce rates of emissions/air
- Procedures to reduce discharge to water

Models of sustainability evaluation are based on approaches that require an economy to appreciate and implement advanced forms of decision making and accountability. It is critical for organizations in developing countries like Egypt to focus on accounting practices that aid decision makers to take into consideration the interests of different stakeholders. Moreover, the sustainable actions that involve entities give high importance to the impact of economic, social, and environmental factors in providing added value and information to stakeholders and reflecting sustainable performance reporting.

Novo Nordisk is a world leader in diabetes care and focuses entirely on health care. The company introduced a way of management in 1997 to ensure integrating sustainable business practices at the operational level (Figure 3.1).

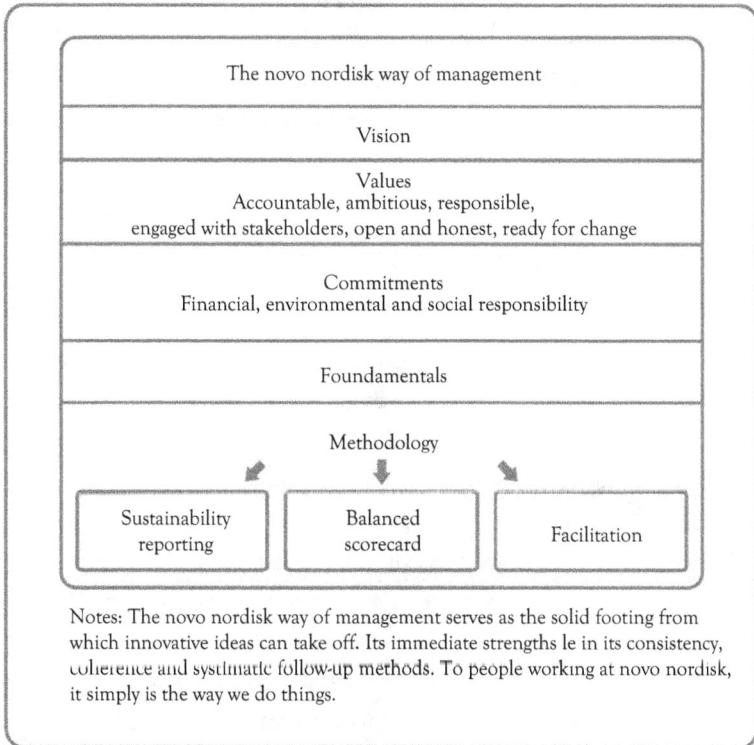

Notes: The novo nordisk way of management serves as the solid footing from which innovative ideas can take off. Its immediate strengths le in its consistency, coherence and systematic follow-up methods. To people working at novo nordisk, it simply is the way we do things.

Figure 3.1 The Novo Nordisk way of management

Source: Adapted from Van Velsor, E., M. Morsing, and D. Oswald. 2009. "Sustainable Leadership: Management Control Systems and Organizational Culture in Novo Nordisk A/S." *Corporate Governance: The International Journal of Business in Society* 9, no. 1, p. 89.

In order to help managers consider sustainability in all of their business decisions, the company has adopted the "Novo Nordisk Way of Management" as an operating tool to help leaders considering sustainability in all of their business decisions. It is based on three pillars:

1. Facilitators who are formed of a team of around 16 high-profile professionals at the holding company working to support sustainability adoption.
2. The annual (sustainability) reporting used to ensure that sustainability thinking becomes part of everyday business practices and to measure its progress toward sustainability by using a *triple bottom line* approach which links a set of key targets to sustainability goals.
3. The balanced score card (BSC) which is the management tool for embedding and cascading the *triple bottom line* approach throughout the organization. The *score card* is a vital element of the corporate governance set-up in Novo Nordisk and thus a very powerful tool to ensure integration of the sustainability approach into all business processes.

Balanced Score Card as a Tool for Internal Sustainability Evaluation

Focus on the environmental and social consequences of organizational practices should form a basis for strategic management of organizational sustainability initiatives as well as its competitive strategies. Eccles and Krzus (2010) discuss concepts and models of integrated reporting by referring to two perspectives. The first one is corporate social responsibility or sustainability reporting, originally referred to as the triple bottom line of economic, environmental, and social metrics. The second is the BSC, which includes financial and nonfinancial metrics. The use of environmental performance indicators has a rather short history in managerial accounting that mostly links to the creation of tools such as the BSC which helps identify critical indicators in recognizing the multidimensional nature of organizational performance.

A strategy-based BSC system aligned with principles of the *triple bottom line* offers a way to accomplish social and environmental goals while integrating them fully with financial performance and competitive advantage. Figure 3.1 illustrates how the same measures used in conventional *BSCs* can incorporate the dimensions necessary for the application of sustainability concepts (Figure 3.2).

To set up a BSC to meet the requirements of sustainable development, a company should implement the following steps:

- Identification of an integrated reporting: management vision of a company's performance; adaptation of issues that define the economic, social, and environmental performance to the company's sustainable strategy
- Setting targets for every aspect of reporting
- Developing and documenting the necessary actions to achieve the proposed objectives
- Developing performance management model linked with company objectives

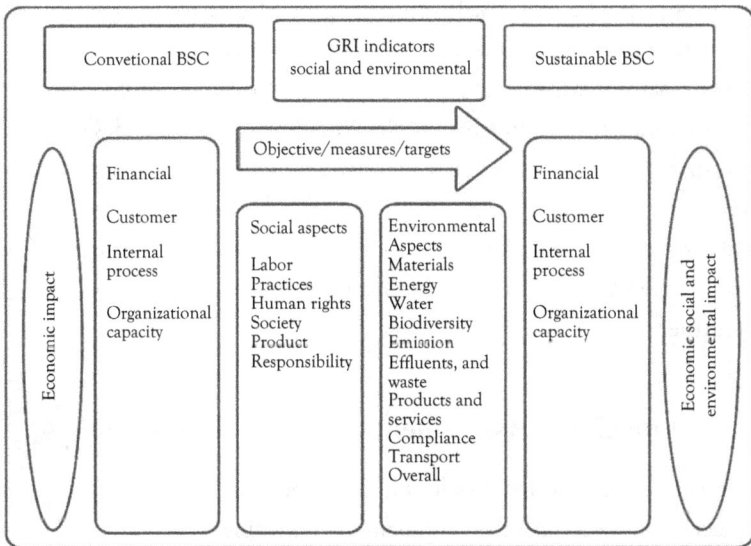

Figure 3.2 Model for integrating social and environmental indicators in BSC

Source: Adapted from Caraiani, C., C.I. Lungu, C. Dascalu, M.V. Cimpoeru, and M. Dinu. 2012. "Social and Environmental Performance Indicators: Dimensions of Integrated Reporting and Benefits for Responsible Management and Sustainability." *African Journal of Business Management* 6, no. 14, p. 4996.

- Designing and implementing an integrated process for assessing integrated (TBL) performance for completion of objectives and actions at least quarterly

The leadership should ensure that labor practices have efficient processes complying with company requirements related to social and environmental aspects. For example, a company becomes more environmentally responsible by verifying CO_2 emissions, green process design, carbon footprint evaluation for products and packaging, testing oil and water for contaminants, checking air quality, assessing noise pollution, achieving EMS certificates, as well as implementing procedures to minimize the risk of corruption within the organization and increase social capital. Social capital refers to the goodwill of key stakeholders and provides a company with the ability to enter local and international markets; it also gives it an enhanced reputation, competitive advantage, cost savings, the ability to charge premium prices, improved relationships with suppliers and distributors, and the ability to attract better talent and goodwill in the eyes of public officials. It can be suggested that the leadership that may determine successful sustainable business is responsible for helping the company to achieve greater economic performance, to be kinder to the environment, and to have a societal positive impact. Besides the BSC as a strategic measurement tool that can be used for measuring sustainability performance, life cycle assessment (LCA) is a system of regulations and certifications frequently used by different companies to demonstrate compliance with sustainability performance standards. This is explained in further detail in the section below.

Life Cycle Assessment a Product Level Tool

Performance indicators should be developed to evaluate sustainability activities undertaken by companies. According to Epstein and Roy (2001) we should translate each sustainability activity into a metric that can be linked to sustainability performance. They highlight three types of activities: (i) formulating the sustainability strategy, (ii) developing plans and programs, and (iii) designing appropriate structures and systems. Moreover, they provide examples for sustainability activities as illustrated in Table 3.1. It shows how the structures and systems come out from strategies which should be formulated by the leaders, for example, adding social and environmental responsibilities as a requirement for senior management positions and also including the formulation of strategies such as emissions reduction.

Table 3.1 Sustainability activities

Sustainability strategy (goals)	Plans and programs	Structure and systems
• Increase the number of facilities with screening procedures against the use of child labor (no. of facilities)	• Investment in cleaner technologies ($)	• ISO 14001 certification labor (no. of facilities)
• Increase gender diversity (% of work force)	• Investment in community projects ($)	• Social performance evaluation systems in place (no. of facilities)
• Reduce lost workdays (no. of days)	• Safety training programs (hours)	• Environmental accounting systems in place (no. of facilities)
• Reduce emissions (% of reduction)	• Support programs for minority-owned business (% of volume of business)	• Senior managers with social and environmental responsibilities (no. of senior managers)

Source: Adapted from Epstein, M.J., and M.J. Roy. 2001. "Sustainability in Action: Identifying and Measuring the Key Performance Drivers." *Long Range Planning* 34, no. 5, pp. 585–604.

Harmful environmental consequences of product manufacturing and usage, the potential prevention of the resulting pollution, as well as exploration of better ways to sustain current resources are generally researched by different groups of academics and practitioners who take into consideration the entire life cycle of the product attempting to come out with useful measures and indicators. There are sustainability performance monitors and measurement indicators used by companies; for example, environment management systems (EMS), International Standards Organization (ISO) 14001 regulations, and European Union Environmental Management and Auditing Scheme (EMAS) include monitoring and measuring mechanisms (Vavra and Ehlova 2012). In order to apply sustainability concepts and practices in companies, a major change or paradigm shift in vision, strategy, and leadership roles should be adopted. It is important, thus, at this stage to elaborate briefly about organizational change and follow that with a detailed account of leadership and leaders in that context.

Conclusion

Measuring sustainable development is not an easy task, because of its complexity and multidimensional concept, the contested nature of the concept of sustainable development itself, and difficulty of measuring many of its components. Sustainable development measures employed a wider range of data than measure of other topics. Governance is measured through composite indicators or "indexes" to capture the multiple facts or dimension of its complex concept. BSC as a tool for internal sustainability evaluation and LCA as a product-level tool are developed using sustainable development measurement based on its different thematic area to assesse sustainable development performance trend for each organization.

CHAPTER 4

Sustainability SMEs

Chapter Objectives

- Subdivide different methods of small and medium enterprises (SMEs) definition.
- Analyze the pillars of sustainability, focusing on the SMEs sector.
- Interpret key factors that influence business sustainability.

The definition of SMEs differs from one country to another, and according to Yu and Bell (2007) "there is no universally accepted definition of an SME" (p. 20). Moreover, they state that the way in which SMEs are defined varies across national statistical systems. For example, Chinese industrial SMEs are defined as those SMEs having less than 2,000 employees, presenting turnover lower than 300 million RMB (i.e., million Euros or 19.2 million GBP), or with total assets lower than 400 million RMB (i.e., 37.6 million Euros or 25.6 million GBP). Compared to the definition of SMEs in other countries, the Chinese classification is more complicated and varies across industrial sectors. Due to the large population in China and the labor-intensive characteristics of the SME sector, China's SMEs tend to be much larger in employee numbers than elsewhere. The Small and Medium Enterprises Policy Development Project report of the Egyptian Ministry of Foreign Trade showed that in developed countries like Canada and the United States the value of the annual sales is used with the number of employees, while countries with transitional economies like Mexico, Thailand, and Turkey mainly define SMEs by the number of employees, and in the European Union, sales, value of assets, and number of employees are used to identify SMEs. According to the same report, the definitions of SMEs in Egypt differ from one entity to another, depending upon their usage, activities, and policy objectives. While there is no agreement upon one operational definition, all definitions include either/or:

1. Number of workers
2. Size of capital
3. The existence of certain legal or institutional conditions

However, the most common used criteria are based on:

1. Number of workers
2. Fixed assets

The Importance of a Unified and Comprehensive Definition of Small and Medium Enterprises

The definition of SMEs gives a comprehensive picture of the country's economy in terms of size, extent of technological development, size of employment, and so on. This is in addition to the importance of unifying the definition and avoiding the multiplicity of laws within a single country. It makes a common language among state agencies, entrepreneurs, and SMEs. It also provides a legislative framework to support them, identifying the entities concerned and obliging them to provide various types of support to small projects.

However, it is important to take into account the importance of periodically renewing the definition within the scope of a single state because of the stages of economic and industrial growth in the economy of the state, in other words, a stage of growth that has its determinants. Since countries vary among themselves in terms of the criteria used to classify SMEs because of their different economies, it is normal for these definitions to differ from one country to the other. This concept also differs between developing and developed countries.

Among the criteria used in the definition of SMEs:

• Number of employees—project management by the owners of the project

- Serving the local market of the state—the degree of risk
- Paid-up capital of the project—the size of the realized net profits
- Annual number of business—technology used

There are two formal definitions of small and micro enterprises in Egypt. The first is mentioned in the text of Law No. 141 of 2004 which states:

> Article (1): In the application of the provisions of this law, a small establishment shall mean every individual company or enterprise engaged in productive, service or commercial economic activity with a paid capital not less than fifty thousand pounds and not more than one million pounds and no more than 50 workers. Article (2): In the application of the provisions of this law, a micro-enterprise shall mean every individual company or enterprise engaged in productive, service or commercial economic activity with a paid-up capital of fifty thousand pounds.

Companies and individual enterprises	Labor size	Capital
Small enterprise	A small project with a maximum of 50 employees	From 50,000 LE and not exceeding 1 million LE
Minor enterprise	That is not stipulated in the text of the law	Less than 50,000 LE

According to ElKhouly and Marwan (2016), the definition of SMEs used by the Ministry of Finance's "Profile of M/SMEs in Egypt" update report submitted by the Environmental Quality International in 2005 was:

- Micro enterprises: one to four workers for all sectors
- Small enterprises: 5–9 workers for trade and service sector and 5–49 for manufacturing, constructions, and others sectors
- Medium enterprises: 10–19 workers for trade and service sector and 50–99 for manufacturing, constructions, and others sectors

The Board of Directors of the Central Bank of Egypt stipulated a definition in its session held on December 3, 2015, which states: Small, medium, and micro enterprises are defined as follows:

	Existing enterprise		Newly established enterprise	
Companies and individual enterprises	Labor size	Capital	Labor size	Capital
Medium enterprise	Less than 200 employees	Less than 1 million LE	Less than 200 employees	Less than 50,000 LE
Small enterprise		From 1 million LE to less than 10 million LE		From 50,000 LE to 5 million LE for industrial establishments and 3 million LE for nonindustrial enterprises
Minor enterprise		From 10 million LE to less than 20 million LE		
Very minor enterprise	Less than 10 employees	From 20 million LE to less than 100 million LE	Less than 10 employees	From 5 million LE to 10 million LE for industrial establishments, and from 3 million LE to 5 million LE for nonindustrial establishments

Unify the Definition of the SMEs in Egypt

The definitions contained in an administrative or ministerial decision will not have the power to modify existing definitions in laws, in application of the principle of legislative precedence, and therefore a uniform universal definition must be enacted by law.

One of the constitutional principles in Egypt states that there are certain important issues that must be determined by law and not by an administrative decision. These include, primarily, crimes, penalties, and taxes, so that the definition will have an effect on tax transactions. It must be stipulated in a law because without this, anyone who adjusts the definition is able to identify and change the tax transactions of those projects, which must remain in the power of Parliament. The author proposes the issuance of a draft law amending the definition of small and micro enterprises with the addition of a definition of medium projects as it is not mentioned in the text of the current law, Law 141/2004.

Egypt is going through stages of economic growth that need to keep abreast of the renewal of the definition of micro, small, and medium enterprises, so we propose that the draft law should postpone the renewal of the definition to the specialized institution, which is assigned to work on the sector of SMEs in Egypt every five years. This definition is binding on all state institutions, which removes us from the legal legislative framework that needs time and effort to adjust, as this does not keep pace with the growing economic movement.

The above makes us wonder which institution is entrusted with dealing with SMEs in Egypt. The research found that there is a multiplicity in these bodies and this multiplicity affects the citizens who seek the service at the end to the dispersion, in addition to the existence of the principle of competition between the donor institutions of finance instead of the principle of solidarity to promote the sector of SMEs in Egypt.

The author suggests the establishment of a single entity for the SMEs in the Egyptian state. Proposals that contain alternatives to the formulation of that body to be an umbrella for the sector become of interest in the sector of SMEs, a national project and not individual support institutions of a country, complementary to each other.

SMEs and Sustainable Development

"Small and Medium-sized Enterprises (SMEs) will play an ever-increasing role in sustainability achievement" (Yu and Bell 2007, p. 20). There are many managers who believe that any ecological efforts in small businesses produce negligible results or that it is the government that should be responsible for issues regarding environmental care. Hobbs (2000) further supports such argument by contending that SMEs are mainly occupied with short-term outcomes and daily issues, rather than with strategic concerns or issues like environmental care and sustainability, due to limited resources in terms of time and manpower as well as financial resources. This further encouraged the author to focus on Egyptian SMEs in his research, especially now with the advent of the 21st century with "climate change and the realization that our natural resources are finite and fast disappearing" (Western 2010, p. 40). Therefore in this research it is suggested that, in order to encourage SMEs which are ignoring sustainable practices to adopt and incorporate them into business strategy, paradigm shifts are needed to allow for change inside firms which is the main task for leaders.

Factors that Influence Business Sustainability

The key driving factors of sustainable practices are shown in Figure 4.1 which shows that corporate image is the most important driver. Other factors, besides improving public image, are government and legislation, personal concern, consumer pressure, supply chain pressure, cost-saving, public pressure, international competitiveness, exploring market opportunities, and employee pressure. The significance of this research is that it attempts to address inherent individual characteristics of sustainability leaders apart from such external pressures and apart from the financial impact on the company as well.

Another external factor regarding sustainability practices relates to how leaders link such practices to financial benefits: many believe that there is no such link or, on the contrary, might believe that such practices

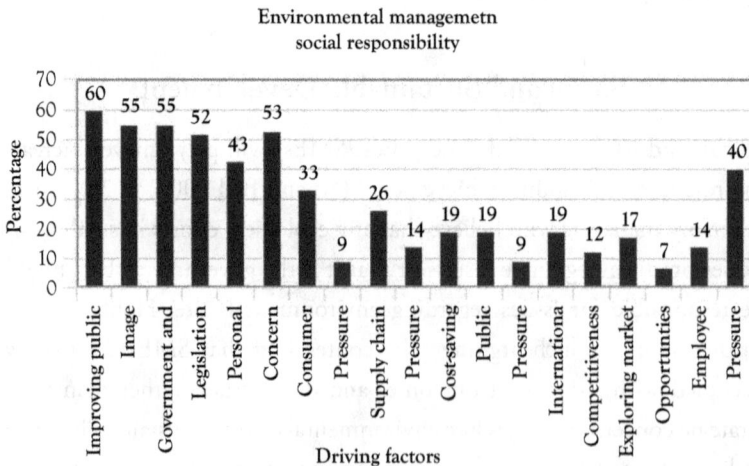

Figure 4.1 Drivers of implementing environmental and social practice

Source: Adapted from Yu and Bell. 2007. "Building a Sustainable Business in China's Small and Medium-Sized Enterprises(SMEs)." Journal of Environmental Assessment Policy and Management 9, no.1, pp. 19–43.

involve unjustifiable costs. This may be due to a lack of knowledge or lack of interest in measuring such financial benefits. One of the main obstacles in implementing business sustainability in SMEs is the fact that leaders of SMEs focus on cash flow and staff availability, which allows them to focus on surviving on a monthly basis and does not allow for time to incorporate sustainability into their strategic thinking.

Moreover, several leaders consider that their companies' environmental impact is very limited and many services or nonmanufacturing companies believe that environmental issues are of no relevancy to their sector. The author, thus, argues that one critical obstacle to implementing business sustainability in SMEs is the leaders' unawareness of the concept. This leads them to neglect environmental and social management issues in their strategic priorities and even neglect thinking that they might have different individual sustainability leaders' characteristics.

Figure 4.2 identifies both driving and resisting forces and an approach to behavior change. It shows the resisting forces that need to be minimized, such as poor ecoliteracy, low environmental awareness, economic barriers, inadequate institutional infrastructure, and limited business support, and driving forces that need to be strengthened, such as education and training, effective research, regulatory framework, and institutional reform (Howarth and Fredericks 2012).

Howarth and Fredericks (2012) used Ghobadian's figure (Figure 4.3) to illustrate the environment-related decision-making elements and processes. Ghobadian's figure offers an overview of some of the key contextual elements and insight(s) to interactions related to SME-environment

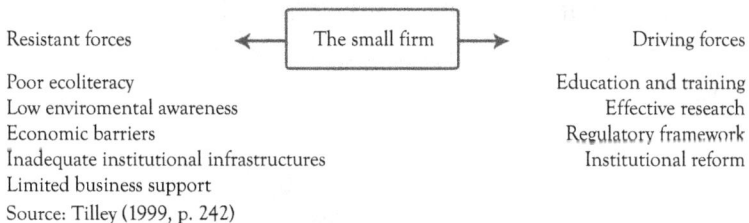

Resistant forces	← The small firm →	Driving forces
Poor ecoliteracy		Education and training
Low enviromental awareness		Effective research
Economic barriers		Regulatory framework
Inadequate institutional infrastructures		Institutional reform
Limited business support		
Source: Tilley (1999, p. 242)		

Figure 4.2 The forces influencing environmental attitudes and behavior of small firms

Source: Adapted from Tilley 1999. "The Gap between the Environment Attitudes and the Environmental Behaviour of Small Firms." *Business Strategy and the Environment* 8, no. 4, p. 242.

Mediating factors   Leadership (style, commitment, concern objectives, etc.)
                              Corporate tradtion
                                 Corporate ethics

External factors	Decision-making process	Enviromental strategies

Market behviour   Technology
Legal-regulatory influences   Opportunity, cost assessment
Social expectation   Human resource availability
                                        Capital availability

Moderating factors   Organisational adaptability

Source: Ghobadian et al. (1998, p. 17)

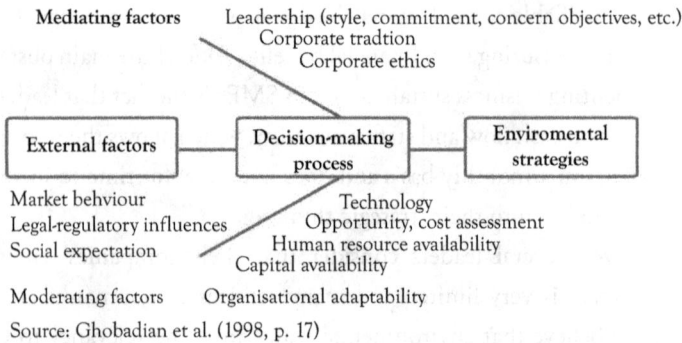

Figure 4.3 Interaction of external

decision-making market behavior, regulatory influences, and social expectation as external factors and the mediating factors which interact to lead decision making in confederations so that the outcomes of this process are ultimately moderated by factors such as opportunity cost assessments and capital and resources availability.

The clear focus to raising attention on environmental issues is based on impacting mediating factors and the important role of exerting pressure, such as the context of Tilley (1999).

Though the above paragraphs highlight many different factors that can influence business sustainability, the objective of this research was to focus on leaders' attributes. It is obvious, though, that among the above-mentioned factors there are those that might influence leaders' attitudes or decisions concerning sustainability issues besides their own attributes. As an example of such factors and as highlighted in Figure 5.1, opportunity, cost assessment, human resource availability, and capital availability act as moderating factors that are suggested to impact the leader's decision. It was thus the role of this research, in the field research phase, to discover those factors, like the ones mentioned above but in the context of the Egyptian culture and norms, that would provide a more comprehensive model as an output of this book.

Conclusion

The importance of sustainability is becoming increasingly marked in the world. It is gradually becoming a very important issue in many countries and within many organizations, especially in developed countries and in large and multinational organizations. SMEs, which represent a major factor in both the economic and environmental impact in different countries, vary in both their awareness and the extent of their application of the sustainability concept and its practices due to different reasons as found in the available literature.

A main factor that can affect SMEs' adoption of sustainability is the leader. Consequently, different studies were done to identify the characteristics of such leaders that can influence their behavior toward environmental sustainability issues and affect the adoption of this concept. Other studies addressed factors that might exert pressure on leaders in favor of or in opposition to the implementation of sustainability practices. It was found that the sustainability concept is taken very lightly in cultures or countries like Egypt, and almost completely neglected in SMEs in these countries. One example that demonstrates such neglect is the lack of training or awareness programs about the importance of the environment and the impact of its sustainability on the future of the planet, and how small changes in our daily workplace activities can highly and collectively impact the retention of different natural resources or prevent polluting the environment.

Regardless of the format of the SME entity, it should be fully responsible for the integrated system that must be provided to SMEs (training and qualification, official paperwork, financial support, marketing, exhibitions, follow-up). Supporting the competent authority for small and medium industrial and nutritious industries for the five main industries, the state is currently directing the Egypt 2030 Strategy by allocating a larger share of funding to support these industries. The state should offer full support for SMEs as they are the nucleus of the economy and the optimal solution to increase domestic output and reduce imports and raise the value of the pound against the U.S. dollar. It is important to invite experts, that too in the field of SMEs, in Egypt to attend youth conferences with special sessions for entrepreneurship and SMEs. It is also important to have a unified definition of SMEs which is binding on all Egyptian state institutions to be renewed every five years depending on the different stages of economic development of the Egyptian state.

In this study the author follows the definition which was stipulated by the Board of Directors of the Central Bank of Egypt in its session as it is the most recent. In addition this book attempts to address an important gap in the Middle East, and in particular in SMEs, that is becoming a global issue and the concern of almost all governments to the extent that it will not be an optional practice in the near future. Therefore the need for studies similar to this one which attempt to identify sustainability leaders' attributes and characteristics in the Middle Eastern culture becomes a necessary if not a pressing issue.

CHAPTER 5

Leaders and Business Sustainability

Chapter Objectives

- Explain simple and practical overview of leadership styles and theories.
- Understand the leader's behavioral approach to business sustainability.
- Provide proposed sustainability leader attributes.

The Leader's Behavioral Approach to Business Sustainability

The sample used by Loewe et al. (2013) in their study was 102 SMEs which were all used for the qualitative analysis. The participants in the sample were asked about the main factors of SME upgrading in Egypt and the main reasons for differences in SME upgrading cases in Egypt. Figure 5.1 shows that the highest two factors pertain to company leader/ owner attributes. This highlights the weight leaders in Egypt have in controlling companies and the direction they take, their growth, and changes.

Moreover, culture was suggested to add more weight to leaders in Egyptian companies, especially company owners and top management, which was what, was understood by leaders in this research. Parnell and Hatem (1999) highlight that in Arab nations the power distance cultural dimension (Hofstede 1980) characterizes the powerful role of being in a superior position, such as a leader (company owner, president in charge,

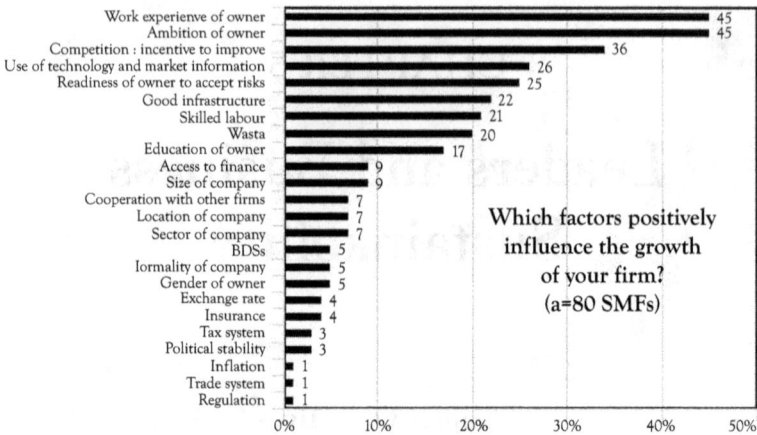

Figure 5.1 Main reasons for differences in SME upgrading ease in Egypt

Source: Adapted from Loewe, M., I. Al-Ayouty, A. Altpeter, L. Borbein, M. Chantelauze, M. Kern, and M. Reda. 2013. "Which Factors Determine the Upgrading of Small and Medium Sized Enterprise (SMEs)?" *The Case of Egypt*

CEO). Due to this power distance cultural dimension, the opinions of someone in a position of higher authority are accepted by default. In such cultures, superiors and those working in subordinate positions are never considered equal and subordinates are always expected to follow orders and be told what to do. The role of power distance in high power index countries like Egypt is that employees are frequently afraid to disagree with their superiors, who are often seen as autocratic or paternalistic. That highlights the role of leaders concerning business sustainability since leaders, owners, and top managers have a great influence and undeniable power in shaping company strategies and their implementation. This led this research to focus on leaders as a main influence for the implementation of business sustainability strategies and processes by virtue of their significant role, power, and control as highlighted above.

Leadership Styles and Theories

The research argues that in order to adequately understand a given leader's attributes, these should be examined in terms of a specific structural context across cultures. Thus, there was a growing need for understanding the way in which leadership is enacted in various cultures and a need for an empirically grounded theory to explain sustainability leader attributes and effectiveness across cultures. Culture influences people of a certain region leading to behavioral norms that not only affect people on an individual level but rather impact the interrelations among them. In this study the author tries to explore how culture might shape or influence the leader as well as the interrelation between the leader and his subordinates.

Minkov and Hofstede (2011) list four distinctive cultural dimensions:

1. Power distance: Social inequality, including the relationship with authority.
2. Individualism–collectivism: The relationship between the individual and the group.
3. Masculinity–femininity: The social implications of having been born as a boy or a girl. (Later editions of the book replaced the word "social" using the word "emotional" instead.)
4. Uncertainty avoidance: Ways of dealing with uncertainty, relating to the control of aggression and the expression of emotions. (Later editions of the book refer to "the extent to which the members of a culture feel threatened by ambiguous or unknown situations.")

Later, pragmatism and indulgence were added to the original dimensions and are defined as follows:

- Pragmatism: "This dimension describes how every society has to maintain some links with its own past while dealing with the challenges of the present and future" (Hofstede 2014).
- Indulgence: "This dimension is defined as the extent to which people try to control their desires and impulses" (Hofstede 2014).

Power distance, individualism, and pragmatism, especially in SMEs where the manager/owner and employees interact more than in large firms, are of particular interest to the Egyptian context. This is particularly relevant to leaders in companies and how the relation with subordinates can be shaped. Moreover, in Egypt SMEs have less formal rules as opposed to other countries and mainly leaders/owners determine the rules to achieve the firm's goals.

El-Kot and Leat (2005) cite a classification carried out by Hofstede (1980) concerning Arab-speaking countries, including Egypt, which demonstrates that such countries have high power distance and low individualism. Moreover Hofstede (2014) classifies Egypt as being low in pragmatism. Figure 5.2 illustrates the above in detail. These dimensions are of particular interest to this research. They interrelate in such a way that shows the importance of leaders when shaping their companies' strategies. This has been further explained where the author discusses power distance, referred to as the acceptance of inequality as the norm.

This section adds more insight on the role of the leader and his/her relationship with subordinates by including the effect of dimensions such as individualism and pragmatism and their interaction with the power distance dimension.

As Figure 5.2 shows, Egypt tends toward being a culture of collectivism, as opposed to individualism, and a culture of very low pragmatism. Collectivists tend to give more importance to group interests than individual interests in that they tend as well to view themselves as part of a bigger family.

This is therefore a significant factor in the Egyptian culture and, combining this with what the power distance dimension refers to, leads us to believe leaders, owners, and top management in this research tend to have

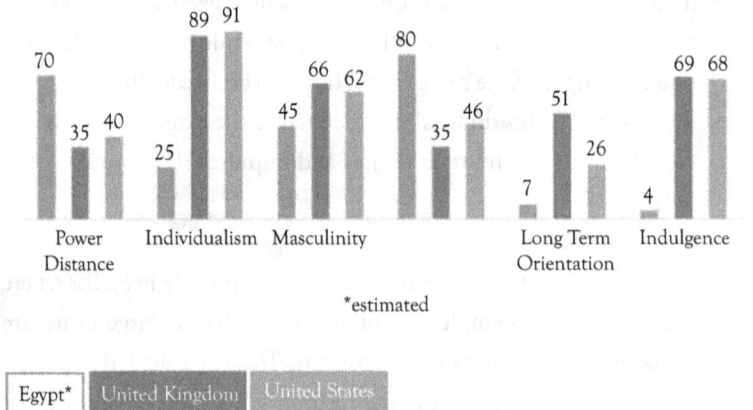

Figure 5.2 A cultural comparison of Egypt with the United States and United Kingdom

Source: (Hofstede 2014)

more influence and control over company strategies and control more than the power distance dimension alone suggests.

As mentioned above, pragmatism refers to maintaining some links with the past (Hofstede 2014). Cultures with low pragmatism such as the Egyptian culture exhibit great respect for traditions demanding unquestionable compliance and respect for superiors in rank or the elderly. Being a religious country, both Muslims and Christians, who make up the totality of Egyptians, treat higher powers with reverence and high respect. Combined with power distance and collectivism, it can be easily suggested that leaders in Egyptian companies, especially in small and medium ones, should be the focus of this research if a significant contribution is to be nurtured when we focus on business sustainability in SMEs in Egypt.

This section lists different historical theories mentioned in the literature reviewed and illustrated in Table 5.1 concerning leadership in general as a necessary introductory step toward better understanding the sustainability leader in particular.

Table 5.1 Brief overview of leadership theories, from "great man" to "complexity leadership"

Great man theories. The great man theory evolved around the mid-19th century (1840)	Based on the belief that leaders are exceptional people, born with innate qualities, destined to lead. The use of the term "man" was intentional since until the latter part of the 20th century leadership was thought of as a concept which is primarily male, military, and western. This led to the next school of trait theories
Trait theories (1930s–1940s)	The lists of traits or qualities associated with leadership exist in abundance and continue to be produced. They draw on virtually all the adjectives in the dictionary which describe some positive or virtuous human attribute, from ambition to zest for life
Behaviorist theories (1940s–1950s).	These concentrate on what leaders actually do rather than on their qualities. Different patterns of behavior are observed and categorized as "styles of leadership." This area has probably attracted most attention from practicing managers

Table 5.1 **(Continued)**

Situational leadership theory (1960s)	Situational. This approach sees leadership as specific to the situation in which it is being exercised. For example, while some situations may require an autocratic style, others may need a more participative approach. It also proposes that there may be differences in required leadership styles at different levels in the same organization
Contingency theory. Proposed in 1967 by Fred Fiedler	This is a refinement of the situational viewpoint and focuses on identifying the situational variables which best predict the most appropriate or effective leadership style to fit the particular circumstances
Transformational theory. The term transformational leadership was first coined by J.V. Downton in *Rebel Leadership: Commitment and Charisma in a Revolutionary Process* (1973). James MacGregor Burns first introduced the concept of transformational leadership in his book *Leadership* (1978)	The central concept here is change and the role of leadership in envisioning and implementing the transformation of organizational performance
Distributed leadership theory. Grom (2000) cites Gibb (1954) as the first author to refer explicitly to distributed leadership theory. He proposes that " leadership is probably best conceived as a group quality, as a set of functions which must be carried out by the group" (Bolden 2011)	Leadership is a process that occurs in groups and involves many leaders
Shared leadership (Pearce and Conger 2003)	Described as "a more robust, flexible and dynamic leadership infrastructure." Though a relatively new concept in organizational literature, shared leadership has recently become the subject of several serious and rigorous studies
Complexity leadership theory. First mentioned in the journal *Emergence: Complexity and Organization*. Issue 8.4, 2006	Leadership in complex systems is an emergent phenomenon that is an outcome of interactions between many people

Source: Adapted from Taylor. 2011. "The Role of Leadership for Environment and Sustainability." *Perspectives on Environment and Sustainability.*

Transformational leadership theory is still the dominant leadership theory, but it is better to use several theories to help understand an aspect of leadership. Some theories are nevertheless more useful in different contexts such as the complexity leadership theory for environmental leadership. Distributed leadership has become a popular leadership theory whereby leadership is conceived of as a collective social process emerging through the interactions of multiple actors. From this perspective, distributed leadership is not something done by an individual to others; it is a group activity, rather than individual action. Bolden (2011) asserts that besides the notion or approach of *distributed leadership* there are other notions as well that help reframe how we understand group leadership. The notion of *shared leadership* has also been in use for some time as have those of *collective leadership, collaborative leadership, co-leadership,* and *emergent leadership*. The common factor across all these accounts is the idea that leadership is not the monopoly or responsibility of just one person, with each suggesting a similar need for a more collective and systemic understanding of leadership as a social process.

The above suggests that the *distributed leadership* concept is useful in supporting business sustainability and, although the author acknowledges Badaracco's (2001) representation of leadership which encourages a shift in focus from the attributes and behaviors of individual leaders to group leaders (a more systemic perspective), due to the newness of the sustainability concept in Egyptian companies, and in SMEs in particular, the author suggests that this study should focus on attributes of individual sustainability leaders as an important antecedent to the notion of group leadership. Group leadership, in the context of sustainability, might be a mature concept and practice in western cultures but not as mature in Middle Eastern cultures nor, particularly, in Egypt. That is an important reason why this research focused on individual attributes rather than on group dynamics. It is very logical to think of group leadership and dynamics as based on individual persons with leaders' attributes or traits that interact together and play a very important role to initiate and maintain any useful organizational change.

Individual leaders who present their vision and ideas in a social and participative manner are, in fact, sharing and socializing their vision rather than imposing or forcing it, hence developing something like a shared cause that ignites passion and drives collective action and behavior all through the organization. In addition such leaders can easily influence, gather, and drive people for higher and sustainable achievements around the core purpose of the organization.

Attributes of individual leaders that may determine successful business sustainability are discussed in the next section.

Sustainability Leader Attributes

According to Visser and Courtice (2011), between the 1920s and the 1960s researchers tried to find some traits as the basis of successful leadership. According to Zaccaro, Kemp, and Bader (2004) the first empirical study of leadership examining the qualities that differentiated leaders from nonleaders produced by Terman (1904) reported such attributes as verbal fluency, intelligence, low emotionality, daring, congeniality, goodness, as well as liveliness as special attributes characterizing youthful leaders. Moreover there are similar studies which burgeoned after Terman's (see Stogdill 1948). "These studies formed the initial empirical backdrop for trait research" (Zaccaro et al. 2004, p. 102). The average person who occupies a position of leadership exceeds the average member of his/her group in the following respects: (i) sociability, (ii) initiative, (iii) persistence, (iv) knowing how to get things done, (v) self-confidence, (vi) alertness to and insight into situations, (vii) cooperativeness, (viii) popularity, (ix) adaptability, and (x) verbal facility (ibid). Zaccaro et al. (2004) categorized different leader attributes to differentiate attributes (cognitive abilities, personality, and motivation values) and proximal attributes (social appraisal skills, problem-solving skills, and expertise/ tacit knowledge). Further supporting this categorization, an empirical summary of leader attributes specified five different categories of attributes as follows: (1) cognitive abilities, (2) personality, (3) motivation, (4) social appraisal and interpersonal skills, and (5) leader expertise and tacit knowledge (Mumford, Zaccaro, Harding, Jacobs, and Fleishman 2000). Attributes of leaders in implementing sustainability and enhancing the level of sustainability in organizations was neglected in numerous studies (Metcalf and Benn 2013; Waldman and Siegel 2008). However, there are studies that tried to find a relationship between leader characteristics and sustainability in organizations (Angus-Leppan, Metcalf, and Benn 2010; Metcalf and Benn 2013; Waldman and Siegel 2008). Although the theory in general is available, this is mainly focused on western culture and there is a lack of studies and development of theories regarding sustainability leadership in Middle Eastern societies. Thus, this research was aimed at discovering attributes of sustainability leaders in a context where there are no previous studies regarding sustainability leadership, therefore addressing an important gap in the literature. Table 5.2 summarizes findings from different studies that tried to find a relationship between leaders' characteristics and attributes and sustainability in organizations.

Shahin and Wright (2004) illustrate the impact of culture on leadership styles in general not taking into consideration sustainability attributes in particular. Their study supports Bass's (1996) contention that Bass and Avolio's (1994) model of transformational and transactional leadership has universal potential. They also mentioned that this model may require adjustment as we move across cultures, arguing that such adjustment was more likely to be required in nonwestern cultures.

Table 5.2 Brief overview of sustainability leader attributes

Sustainability leader competencies: A grounded theory study (Schwalb 2011)	This study has looked at leaders' traits/qualities/characteristics/competencies
	Finding: Grounded theory model of sustainability leader competencies.
	Five core dimensions of leader competencies resulted from participant reports:
	(1) knowledge, (2) skills, (3) style, (4) method, and (5) mission-critical
	1. Knowledge: Knowledge in areas of business, economics, markets, human behavior, decision processes, and community life were viewed as fundamental to those who would lead a sustainability initiative or organization
	2. Skills: Communication, dealing with ambiguity, building, and maintaining relationships, dealing with complexity, project management, and conflict resolution are examples of skills deemed important to be learned and developed
	3. Style: Style refers to leadership style, which describes the behavior of a leader. Northouse (2010) says the style focuses exclusively on what leaders do and how they act
	4. Method: Method has to do with "how" an individual should lead
	5. Mission-critical: Dutra et al. (2011) describe mission-critical competencies as having the ability to see multiple futures

Table 5.2 **(Continued)**

Sustainability leadership: Linking theory and practice. "Cambridge Sustainability Leadership Model" (Visser and Courtice 2011)	This research was concerned in locating sustainability within the leadership literature, defining the concept of sustainability leadership, and presenting a model of sustainability leadership in practice. The model presents insights into sustainability leadership in three areas: context, individual characteristics, and actions. The individual characteristics are: a. Caring/morally driven: Are for the well-being of humanity and all other forms of life, as well as being guided by a moral compass b. Systemic/holistic thinker: The ability to appreciate the interconnectedness and interdependency of the whole system, at all levels, and to recognize how changes to parts of the system affect the whole c. Enquiring/open-minded: Actively seeking new knowledge and diverse opinions, questioning received wisdom, including being willing to have one's own opinions challenged d. Self-aware/empathetic: High levels of emotional intelligence (the ability to understand their own emotions and those of others), sincerity, personal humility, and reflexiveness (the ability to see their own place in and influence on a situation) e. Visionary/courageous: Sustainability leaders bring inspiration, creativity, optimism and courage to bear in the role, driven to produce results and possess the ability to balance passion and idealism with ambition and pragmatism.
Sustainability managers or rogue mid-managers? "A typology of corporate sustainability managers" (Tang et al. 2011)	This study demonstrates that deeper investigation into corporate sustainability at the level of the individual gives us a more holistic view of sustainability management and a broader vision of why it is important Findings: It identifies four categories of sustainability managers: scientist, messenger, artist, and storyteller The findings suggest the key role of expertise, empowerment, values, inspiration, strategic thinking, and social contribution as key meaning for these managers. The empirical findings help build on understanding the different psychological dimensions of corporate sustainability management and provides a useful tool for developing effective organizational leadership, enhancing recruitment and retention of sustainability talent, and improving individual and team performance for key sustainability growth
Sustainability and authentic leadership: Stumbling blocks and enablers (Lombard et al. 2012)	Finding: Model of stumbling blocks and enablers of authenticity An authentic leadership development strategy is urgently needed for leaders to cope with the ethical issues faced in order to achieve sustainability in leadership Definitions of authenticity: Within the assignments, participants were asked to draw on published academic definitions of authenticity and to choose the definition which best reflected their own personal perspectives. The 210 submissions were manually grouped into 5 themes and categories. The categories which emerged were *authenticity and trust*, *authenticity and self-awareness*, *authenticity and relationships*, *authenticity and the perception of others*, and *authenticity and balance*. These form the basis for an overall understanding of authenticity and leadership

The relationship between transformational leadership and organizational sustainability (Ghaem 2013)	The main finding of the study: There is a positive relationship between transformational leadership and the sustainability of an organization According to Bass (1990), transformational leader characteristics are : a. Charisma: Provides vision and sense of mission, instills pride, gains respect and trust b. Inspiration: Communicates high expectations, uses symbols to focus efforts, and expresses important purposes in simple ways c. Intellectual stimulation: Promotes intelligence, rationality, and careful problem solving d. Individualized consideration: Gives personal attention, treats each employee individually, coaches, and advises
Others	According to surveyed leaders, the three most critical individual leadership competencies necessary for adopting triple bottom line approaches are long-term view, communication, and influence (Quinn and Baltes 2007). Some other key attributes that may be important to leadership behavior are enthusiasm, energy, confidence, propensity to focus on communication, and so on (Taylor 2011). The shift from centralized leadership style to decentralized, shared leadership style is important because, according to Pearce et al. (2013), shared leadership highly impacts sustainability outcomes in organizations in different contexts. Moreover, they also found that decentralized, shared leadership is more effective than centralized leadership in influencing the citizenship behavior of different employees. Self-leadership and thinking style may be important attributes which is supported by Prussia, Anderson, and Manz (1998) who found a relationship between self-leadership strategies, self-efficacy, and performance. Moreover Dutra et al. (2011) refer to how CEOs make decisions by using available information to reach assumptions that guide them in making such decisions and further articulate about how such managers finally reach decisions, demonstrating the complexity and interdependency of different pieces of information that leaders should process in order to make sound decisions in the context of the required sustainability outcomes

Moreover, Shahin and Wright (2004) highlight different categories of leader attributes that may apply to the Egyptian culture:

- Positive leadership that includes items relating to respect, morality, power, direction, checking, reward, collective mission, and strong sense of mission
- Enthusiastic leadership, which reflects seeking different perspectives to solve problems, suggesting new ways of looking at how to do work, expressing confidence in work, and talking enthusiastically about what should be accomplished

- Social integration, which reflects encouragement of social gatherings due to the importance of this at work and for the achievement of work objectives, and encouraging group members to discuss work issues together
- Authoritarian leadership, which reflects enjoying exercising power and influencing group members
- Individual consideration, which reflects teaching and coaching, treating subordinates as individuals, and considering them as having different needs, abilities, and aspirations

Egyptian Culture and Leaders' Attributes

In light of the influence that culture exerts on leader attributes it is worth mentioning that Egyptians believe that their deep ancient historical roots will somehow lead them into a new civilization. Shahin and Wright (2004) remark that ancient Egypt was ruled by one person, the *Pharaoh*, assisted by a top executive and the government council. Subsequent political systems in Egypt show remarkably similar characteristics. Under Arab Islamic rule Egypt was again controlled by one person, the *Wali* who controlled the executive and judicial functions, the leadership of the army and the police. In 1952, Egypt became a presidential state. The president has dominant political and governmental authority.

Family plays a central role in the Middle East countries. In a survey conducted in Egypt, Egyptians were found to have a great fear of loneliness; they always desire to be surrounded by relatives and friends. That explains why social integration inevitably has a major influence on Egyptian working life. Such argument suggests that the findings of this research might lead to attributes such as giving personal attention, coaching, and advising. Egypt has a large majority of Sunni Muslims and a small minority of Christians, with the majority of Christians being Coptic Orthodox and the rest being Protestants and Roman Catholics. Egyptians take their parents' religion. In such a religious culture, the findings of this research might lead to attributes such as honesty, modesty, exemplary, committed optimism, resiliency, transparency, and ethics.

Conclusion

It can be easily suggested that since every culture has its special characteristics, researching sustainability leaders' attributes individually in different cultures becomes an important requirement to enrich such a field of research and further establishes the importance of the study at hand, given that the Egyptian culture is lacking in such research efforts.

CHAPTER 6

"Sustainability Leader Attributes" New Model

Chapter Objectives

Provide new model to illustrate the sustainability leader attributes and dimensions of measuring sustainability performance (Figure 6.1).

The qualitative analysis from the in-depth interviews developed a conceptual framework for the leader's attributes (attitude, behavior, and competencies) that may determine successful business sustainability in terms of the environment for SMEs in Egypt (Figure 6.1). After data collection and analysis three factors emerged that have a correlation effect on sustainable SMEs: (1) sustainability leader, (2) firm capabilities, and (3) governmental policies. The major factor is sustainability leader. Eight major thematic categories emerged for the sustainability leader attributes. Three dimensions measuring SME sustainability performance emerged. Before data collection the author expected that SMEs leaders would be mainly concerned with sustainability as an additional cost with no significant benefits to the business. After data collection, this perception had slightly changed. It was observed that some of the participants considered implementing sustainability concepts which, apart from being a charitable deed, can be a source of opportunities and competitive advantage.

While the participating companies have already undertaken activities to improve society and the environment, these efforts have not been nearly as productive as they could be. This was especially observed during the author's visits to those companies; for example, two of the companies choose suppliers who use raw materials that are not environmentally harmful and which have recycling programs for their waste. Some of the companies hoped to implement environmental-friendly programs but

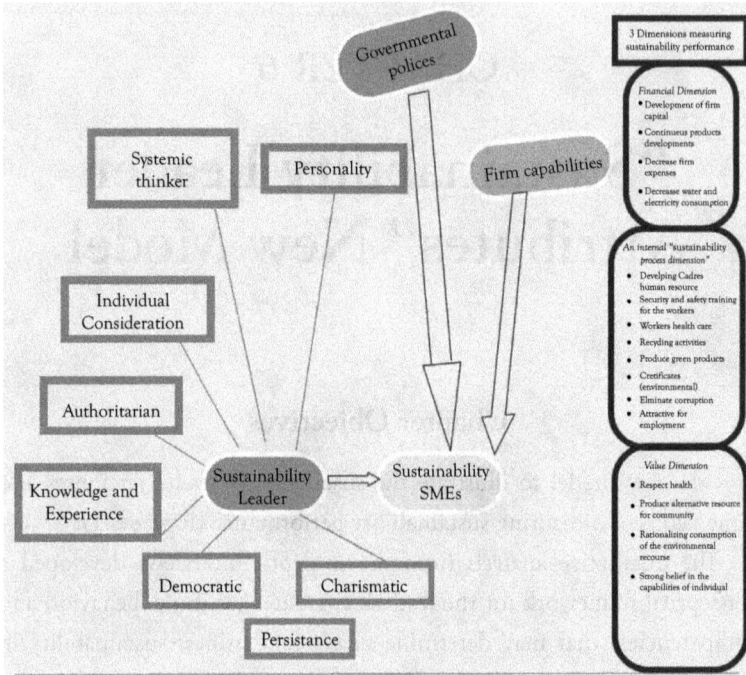

Figure 6.1 **New model illustrate the sustainable leader attributes and dimensions of measuring sustainability performance**

lacked actual activities. This was further evidenced through their use of the word "they" instead of "I" or "we" during the interviews. There are no significant differences between the Turkish company and the other Egyptian companies, especially companies which have the same industrial nature and the same classification for sustainability performance measurement. One considered the size of his business as not big enough to take social and environmental responsibilities and considered taking that role in case his company became larger. The above points might imply that SMEs leaders believe that sustainability concepts are much more feasible in larger companies than they are in smaller ones. The researcher concluded that the business sustainability concept is new for Egyptian SMEs. Awareness campaigns are required for this concept to be effectively incorporated in business strategies and operations.

Eight categories were used to create a framework in order to answer the following question: "What are the leaders attributes (attitude, behavior, and competencies) that may determine successful business sustainability in terms of the environment for SMEs?"

In addition to leaders' attributes, three different sustainability performances measurement dimensions emerged: financial, internal sustainability process dimension, and value dimension. Two of these dimensions match with two of the conventional balanced score card (BSC) aspects (financial and internal process dimensions) mentioned in the literature review chapter (Figure 3.1, Section 2.3.1). This is supported by Wisner, Epstein, and Bagozzi (2006) when they summarized the different dimensions that can be used to create BSC for sustainability reporting results as follows:

- Financial dimension (sales revenues from sustainable products, energy cost saving, and the avoidance of the future regulatory cost)
- An internal business process dimension (supplier certification and toxic or hazardous waste reduction)
- Stakeholder dimension (customer and community satisfaction; awards received for green/sustainability practices; charitable donations to environmental organizations)
- A learning and growth dimension (sustainability-trained employee, hours volunteered to the community, and environmental projects employee)

The BSC sustainability performance measurement was used as a basis for selecting the SMEs participants in the study where applying at least one of the BSC model-mentioned dimensions renders an SME feasible for the theoretical sample.

Phenomenological experience related to sustainability leader attributes. These antecedents had eight categories: systemic thinking, individual consideration, authoritarian, expertise and knowledge, persistence, charismatic, democratic, and personality. Each is discussed in detail below.

Systemic Thinking

Literature showed that strategic thinking plays an important role in strategic management, strategic development, and strategic planning. However, there is no clear or common definition for the strategic thinking term. Zabriskie and Huellmantel (1991) argue that it is important to detect the prompt description of strategic thinking.

In this study, systemic thinking was a major category during the open coding phase. It encloses recovering direction detractions to goals, and the logical and systemic following of rules as well as commitment to them.

The majority of participants in this study felt that the systemic thinking attribute was a requirement for sustainability leaders. For example, the CEO of one of the companies said, "The adaption of environmental sustainability activities needs logical and systemic following rules."

In order to cope with the advancements in a modern business environment, The organization needs to increasingly adopt strategic concepts and take advantage of qualified strategic thinkers. Thus, thinking strategically necessitates thinking techniques, thinking concepts, thinking styles, and thinking skills (Hanford 1995).

Moreover, for a company to manage future difficult situations, it has to depend on a clear strategic vision and how to achieve its goals.

From the above, we can suggest that business leaders require the strategic thinking attribute to set strategic plans for their business, the application of goals of their strategic plans, and strategic management. Concomitantly, Sveiby (2001) said that "knowledge-based strategy formulation starts with the competence of people." Thus, the research focused on capacities and qualities which are necessary to achieve strategic management tasks.

The conclusion history Table 5.2 illustrates competences and skills required for performing strategic managerial tasks which were stated in the review literature.

A longitudinal study was carried out depending on interviews with 35 senior executives attributed to 35 of the 100 largest Australian organizations between the mid-1980s and mid-1990s, interrogating their opinions in variations in the processes of strategic planning, strategic management, and corporate development. The interview focused on the

Andrews (1971)	Rowe & et al., (1986)	Mintaberg (1994)	Thomson & Strickland (1996)	Heracleous (1998)	Liedtka (1996)	Graetz (2002)	Boon (2005)
Analytical conceptual			Analytical Conceptual Visionary				
	Visionary Creativity Flexibility Entrepreneurship	Visionary Creativity		Creativity		Creativity	Visionary Creativity
		Synthesis	Synthesis	Synthetics		Synthetics	
			Knowlege	Divergent		Divergent	Systemic thinking
					System Perspective		
					Intent Focus Thinking on time Hypothesis driven Acting in intelligent manners		
		Intuitive				Intuitive	

problems they faced during their work regarding strategic planning and strategic management tactics five years before (Nuntamanop et al. 2013).

Strategic thinking was one of the main problems faced regardless of whether the company adopted a formalized strategic planning approach or used a no formalized one.

"Our senior executives tend to get carried away by details and lose their strategic perspective" was an example of a phrase stated by a senior executive in a formalized strategic planning system company (Nuntamanop et al. 2013).

Garratt (1995a) shows that the lack of strategic thinking is worldwide, not only in Australia, but also in London, Europe, East Asia, New Zealand, and the United States. He elaborated, adding "Around 90% of managers and vice-presidents had no induction, inclusion or training to become a competent direction giver of their business." Bonn (2001) discovered that absence of strategic thinking leads to lack of better decisions and value-adding processes. However, if strategic thinking is present, better corporate decisions would have been made and greater value provided to constituents.

There is a clear difference between strategic thinking and strategic planning as they represent different stages in the strategy development process.

> Since, Strategic planning focuses on analysis and deals with the articulation, elaboration and formalization of existing strategies, Strategic thinking—on the other hand—emphasizes on synthesis, using intuition and creativity to create an integrated perspective of the enterprise. (Mintzberg 1994)

Mintzberg also suggests that strategic thinking precedes strategic planning.

Garratt (1995b) defined strategic thinking as a procedure which senior executives use to deal with daily managerial activities and emergencies. Moreover, Liedtka (1998) argues that strategic thinking has been known as an individual activity influenced by the framework of the organizations. The literature mentioned a number of major notions of strategic thinking: it is an essential element for strategic planning and strategic development and that it has a mental mechanism, perspectives, and actions. This agrees with the point of view that strategic thinking and strategic planning are two different hypotheses. In addition, Liedtka supports the concept that strategic thinking is a process which comes first before strategic thinking.

Over the past 25 years, studies showed that there was a difference between strategic thinking and operational thinking. Strategic thinking leads to an interruption of long-term and analytical planning activities, while operational thinking is issues and tasks oriented (Honford 1995). According to Tovstiga (2010), strategic thinking might occur all the time before, during, or after strategic planning and operation stages.

As Chatman et al. (1986) have argued:

> When we look at individual behavior in organizations, we are actually seeing two entities: the individual as himself and the individual as a representative of this collectivity ... Thus the individual is not only acting on behalf of the organization in the usual agency sense, but he is also acting, more subtly "as the organization" when he embodies values, beliefs, and goals of the collectivity.

Thus we can suggest that there are two different levels of strategic thinking: the individual level and the organizational level. That may open an argument about the influence effect of the individual characteristics, thinking, and behavior, and how they can influence the organization culture and performance, while, on the other side, there is the influence of the organizational context on individual thinking and behavior.

From the above, we can suggest that understanding strategic thinking necessitates two approaches that explore the character of a strategic thinker and the culture and actions that take place within the organizational context which the individual controls (Nuntamanop et al. 2013). Thus, to find a near true picture of the effects of different leadership attributes on sustainability development in the SMEs, the researcher looked at their impact on individual leaders and on the approach by which they influence their surrounding wider organizations, mood, environment, activities, culture, and structure.

Individual Consideration

Individual consideration was formerly conceptualized as the surrounding support and personalized concentration utility. The second category is individual consideration which involves caring about others. Participants refer to the individual consideration attribute by certain codes, including transferring ideas to others, inspiring others, the ability to discover skills in others, the ability to develop skills in others, and persuading others. Moreover, employees training involvement, observing employees' skills development, challenged delegation tasks, career advancement, discovering employees' needs, and knowing suitable motivational tools need to be considered by the leader for each employee. We have seen a move to define individual consideration as concomitant with servant leadership. This was supported by Avolio and Bass (1995) when they stated that a "leader displays more frequent individualized consideration by showing general support for the efforts of followers." Rafferty and Griffin (2006) studied the similarities and dissimilarities between developmental and supportive scopes of individual consideration, in addition to focusing on discovering the supportive leadership style which is defined as "occurring when leaders express concern for, and take account of, followers' needs and preferences when making decisions." Developmental leadership includes support for training, career counseling, and examining and monitoring employees' skill improvement (Rafferty and Griffin 2006).

The above highlights the importance of better understanding of this attribute and how it is practiced by leaders on a daily basis.

In order to be a sustainability leader having the individual consideration attribute, which is an assignment and not an honor, one may be required to put employees' needs above one's own. For example, in terms of support, the leader will spend time and effort to develop an employee if there is a training opportunity and if it is limited, a leader might promote an employee to a training opportunity versus going himself/herself (Arnold and Laughlin 2010).

A grounded theory study about transformational leadership behaviors in the context of Indian culture, conducted by Singh and Krishnan (2005), revealed a special apparatus that arose from their data, "self-sacrifice." The grounded theory approach is limited for studying transformational leadership. In addition, self-sacrifice is an important characteristic of transformational leadership, not only in the Indian context, but also in other cultures like North America. Self-sacrifice in an organizational setting was defined as "the total/partial abandonment, and/or permanent/temporary postponement of personal interests, privileges, or welfare in the division of labor, distribution of rewards, and/or exercise of power" (Choi and Mai-Dalton 1999).

From the studies emerged an active factor which may affect individual consideration and self-sacrifice; this factor is leader gender. It is suggested that female leaders may experience more confrontation than male leaders in being perceived as exemplary leaders. Moreover, studies showed that individualized consideration is significantly more correlated with femininity than masculinity (Arnold and Laughlin 2010). For example, van Knippenberg's (2005) study found that individual consideration (e.g., a supervisor's enthusiasm to take on a larger part of the workload, to give up a day off in favor of a follower) is most necessary for the effectiveness of leaders who are not ideal in their groups. In addition, their study showed that female leaders are believed to require connection in more group-oriented (i.e., individual consideration) behavior to demonstrate their commitment to the group and be authorized as leaders. According to Eagly and et al., (2003), meta-analytic studies showed that female leaders seem to endorse individual consideration more frequently than male leaders. In order to connect a theory building implement related to refining construction of individual consideration, the author conducted interviews with senior SMEs leaders across the private sector, because they had a rich background, experience, and history of practicing leadership in general and individual consideration specifically. Yet at the same time, the lack of conceptual clarity around the sustainability leader attributes suggested a grounded approach to theory development. Because of these considerations, the research utilized a blended grounded theory method in order to "bring a new perspective and new theorizing to [this] mature established theoretical area" (Locke 2001, p. 97). The individual consideration attribute is one of the constructions that emerged from the grounded approach.

Authoritarian

Authoritarian leaders probably employ control by setting structure, ground rules, and promising rewards for fulfillment and intimidating punishment for defiance or breaking the rules (Aryee et al. 2007). The literature suggests that SMEs leaders prefer to control and supervise each activity by their own interactions (Be dell et al. 2006). This led to the suggestion that managers' authoritarian leadership in turn influences their employees' performance (Schuh et al. 2013). This was supported by Aryee (2007) as he argued that an authoritarian leadership style is to be allied with employees' perceptions of critical tasks which require full supervision.

In the research under study, the participants proposed that leaders at the application phase of adopting sustainability activities should use their authority power, for example, by making decisions with little or no participation or creative input from their subordinates or team members and directly supervised group members. The authoritarian attribute is important in the industrial field where decisions need to be made effectively and efficiently.

From the subordinates' point of view, violence and leader's personal benefits are always associated with absolute power (Sivanathan et al. 2008). Authoritarian leaders' willingness to declare their personal supremacy over employees and control employees' performance primarily via threats and intimidation makes them especially likely to be perceived as abusive, as also using behaviors which highlight unilateral decision making by the leader and endeavoring to maintain the distance between the leader and his/her subordinates (Aryee et al. 2007). In addition, they believe that authoritarian leadership behavior belongs to the old school of management which is centralization management. Moreover, a number of scholars have suggested that authoritarian leadership behaviors indicate a strong disregard for the benefit and point of view of their subordinates (Chan et al. 2012). For example, authoritarian leaders tend to pay no attention to subordinates' ideas and ignore their inputs in the decision-making process (Aryee et al. 2007). However, managers see that authoritarian leaders who use power with their subordinates guarantee accuracy of doing business tasks and activities (Tsui et al. 2004).

These behaviors guarantee the leader's authority over the path of the team directing them to achieve his/her objectives. Specifically, authoritarian leadership has been defined as "leader's behavior that asserts absolute authority and control over subordinates and [that] demands unquestionable obedience from subordinates" (Schuh et al. 2013).

White and Lippitt (1960) acknowledged the autocratic leader as the authoritarian leader. Other literature has cited that "autocratic leader" and "authoritarian leader" have the same meaning without distinguishing between them (Schuh et al. 2013). Authoritarian leaders depend on their power to force and their ability to influence (Bass 1990).

Persistence

The participants proposed that the leader in the initial phase of adopting the sustainability concept needs to make his/her team members (employees) aware of it. As they become aware, the leader must be persistent through the implementation phase. The leader should take on the role of planning, organizing, and mentoring. Finally, the leader must be patient and resolute (Schwalb 2011).

Holland and Shepherd (2013) defined entrepreneurial persistence as moments "when the entrepreneur chooses to continue with an entrepreneurial opportunity regardless of counterinfluences or enticing alternatives."

Williams (2017) showed that many factors affect entrepreneurs' persistence. Besides individual factors, environmental and situational factors (e.g., difficult and unconventional opportunities) (Holland and Shepherd 2013) and uncertain financial, competitive, and operational environments (Liao and Gartner 2006) influence entrepreneurs' choices to persist. Thus persistence is based on both the individual entrepreneur and the environment (DeTienne et al. 2008).

McMullen and Shepherd (2006, p. 134) defined entrepreneurial action, which is crucial for entrepreneurial persistence, as "behavior in response to a judgmental decision under uncertainty about a possible opportunity for profit." Persistence helps start-up companies to survive (Gartner and Shaver 2012). One of the factors that increase persistence is when entrepreneurs follow specific activities (e.g., gestation activities).

Liao and Gartner (2006) confirmed that early planning leads to persistence in ambiguous situations.

Thus, entrepreneurial persistence research progression focuses mainly on understanding the methodology of its application rather than just defining it.

Charismatic

It is known from literature that charismatic leadership probably takes place in situations that are vague and stressful for the employees and the company (Yukl 1999). By their attitudes and actions, charismatic leaders push employees to accomplish big objectives (Dvir et al. 2002). Charismatic leadership gives rise to ethical matters. The purpose of leadership is the main norm for assessing the ethical manners of the charismatic leader (Paulsen et al. 2009).

The leader needs to be charismatic to support team dynamics and practices to build a sense of character that encourages the required sense of society, belief, and teamwork to turn sustainability concepts and theories into innovative products and activities in their companies (Keller 2006; Somech 2006). The charismatic leader motivates employees with their own self-belief and communicates the logic of purpose and vision (Howell and Shamir 2005). Compared with other leadership styles, charismatic leaders boost employees' efficacy as they encourage a belief in the company's vision and inspire belief in team members' skills (Keller 2006).

All participants had at least two codes within this category. From the participants' point of view, the sustainable leader should be charismatic and the charisma will be built when the leader is trustable, is modest, has consistency, and is an exemplar in applying the sustainability concept in the firm by treating employees equally as much as possible. The leader should be authentic in action and speech and demonstrate the kind of behavior that he would like to see (Paulsen et al. 2009). Moreover, the leader should answer the question, what the firm would like to achieve in the future or what we aspire to be in the future; thus, he should be a visionary.

Paulsen et al. (2009) found that there was significant correlation between charismatic and coaching leadership and employees' outcomes.

Figure 6.2 illustrates an integrative conceptual model of the relationship between charismatic leadership, team identity, cooperation, and team innovation. The framework emphasizes that charismatic leadership affects team identity, while team identity endorses cooperation within groups.

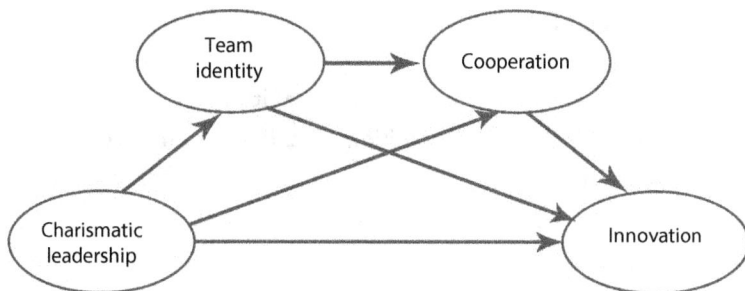

Figure 6.2 Expertise and Knowledge

Expertise and Knowledge

Expertise and knowledge refer to the leader beliefs; they include the awareness of the leader toward globalization and sustainability concepts and whether the leader has a background about sustainable development. Participants suggested that the leader should be well educated, a continuous learner, and well cultured.

For leaders gathering knowledge, it is very important that the knowledge is about their industry and business activities, which will make a positive impact on their companies. An initial logic embraces a belief that effective, knowledgeable and expert leaders support modern business concepts which positively influence instructional practices and learning opportunities for all employees (Steven 2014).

The concept of knowledgeable leader formation has conclusively found a target population in the sphere of business (Nonaka 1991). As leaders in knowledge construction processes convert data into knowledge, the resulting suggestion supports well-versed decision making in SMEs, and knowledge conception was considered an important process on the part of SMEs and sustainability leaders (Katz et al. 2009). In the organization environment, knowledge was created as leaders' synthesized information by illustration of their values and understandings and was equipped for action (Breiter and Light 2006). As the leaders formed and shared knowledge with others at diverse levels of the company, knowledge was augmented and mobilized, as knowledge is stimulated through individuals and clusters (Robinson 1995). For example, the importance of expertise and knowledgeable leaders was highlighted as they played an arbitration role between the vision of the company and the realities of those working on the front line—the "employees" (Steven 2014).

Taking into consideration a learning area, it fundamentally also represents an essential leadership position by endorsing knowledge formation within the factors of the area as set out by structure leaders, actions that take place on a day-to-day basis without consciousness, and the specific context of the company. A development of organizational learning arises when the contemporary knowledge of leaders becomes an element of the organization.

To explore knowledge within a company culture, it is necessary to think that employees bring values and actions to the information arising from the company environment.

As knowledge influencers, leaders had to guarantee that newly acquired knowledge in the company did not stay remote from actions (Steven 2014).

According to Nonaka and Takeuchi (1995), knowledge influencers were defined as

> leaders, who have access to knowledge creating groups at the local and system level. Beyond acting as conduits to move knowledge between teams and levels of the organizations, a process of cross-leveling, knowledge influencers actively engaged in the knowledge creation process within teams.

Also, the practical experience which promotes effective leaders is very important. York-Barr and Duke (2004) proposed that leaders' expertise can be followed from the individual stage to the collaborative stage through skilled leaders sharing effective practices.

In this research, expert and knowledgeable leaders supported shared efforts that allowed the exchange of knowledge, information, experiences, and skills between all the company levels. One of the leader roles is to maintain knowledge mobilization processes in their company and not to prevent any experience or knowledge from moving between teams and different levels of the company. According to Steven (2014), "These linkages between levels of the company presented opportunities to bypass possible learning cycle breakdowns such as fragmented learning."

From the field work, most subordinates surely highlighted the participation of leaders in sharing work, bringing to the team different perceptions; thus they were knowledge influencers.

Example discussions follow for the data selection phase (at the in-depth interviews) with well-educated expertise participants (SMEs owners).

The author opened a discussion about the basic steps in strategic planning for applying environmental sustainability activities.

Answer:

One of them said:

Any company that determines it is indeed ready to begin strategic planning must perform four tasks to cover the way for a planned, controlled, and structured process:

1. Identify specific objectives.
2. Clarify roles (who do what in the process).
3. Develop organizational benefits and outcomes.
4. Identify the resources and information that must be collected to help make sound decisions.

Author one mentioned:

Before starting on the basic steps in a strategic plan for applying environmental sustainability activities, we must first answer the questions below:

- Purpose—why should the company apply environmental sustainability activities? And what does it seek to accomplish?
- Business—The main method or activity through which the company tries to fulfill this purpose.
- Values—the principles or beliefs that guide company members as they pursue the company's purpose.

He continued once a company has been committed to why it should apply environmental sustainability activities and what it seeks to accomplish, identifying a clear method answers about how it can apply the objectives. For this it must take a clear look at its current situation. Remember that a part of strategic planning, thinking, and management is an awareness of resources and an eye to the future environment, so that a company can successfully respond to changes in the environment. Situation assessment, therefore, means obtaining current information about the company's strengths, weaknesses, and performance—information that will highlight the critical issues that the company faces and that its strategic plan must address. These could include a variety of primary concerns, such as funding sustainability issues, new environmental sustainability activities, and changing regulations or changing needs in the client population. The point is to choose the most important issues to address.

Democratic

Since leadership plays an essential role in modern business activity movements, understanding the features of democratic leadership is vital (Choi 2007). However, the definition of democratic leadership is unclear (Gastil 1994).

According to White and Lippitt (1960), democratic leadership

> Emphasizes group participation, discussion, and group decisions encouraged by the leader. On the other hand, an autocratic leader keeps tight control over group decisions and activities. The autocratic leader determines all policies, techniques, and activity steps and dictates the particular work tasks and work companions of each member.

Thus we can say that the vital trait of democratic leadership is sharing and participation; they are a basic function of democratic leadership (Choi 2007).

Also, the leadership literature has paid no attention to democratic leadership in the context of environmental sustainability in Egypt within small groups and organizations. In this study, the participants said that attribute is important at the initial phases when the leaders are ready to prioritize training and team development and take the time needed to give everyone a chance to contribute. The employees share the responsibility for making decisions and changes for a sustainable environment. The leader effectively communicates with his employees, respects others, builds positive relations with the work force, delegates a great deal of the work, seeks regular feedback, and looks to create a harmonious and productive work force.

Personality

It is known that personality is assumed to be quite stable over time, mostly in adults. Studying personality is beneficial in improving our understanding of particular character. Scholars have suggested a limitation of employing a person-centered approach to personality research (Merz and Roesch 2011).

Referring to leaders' variation in competences models of thoughts, beliefs, and attitudes, researches of personality focus on understanding leaders' differences in particular personality characteristics, such as friendliness.

Innovative, honest, and ambitious were suggested by the participants to be personal attributes for the sustainability leader. The participants' suggestion input identifies leaders with similar levels in the rest of their personality characteristics and define their character profiles.

Conclusion

Eight categories were used to create a framework in order to answer the following question: "What are the leaders attributes (attitude, behavior, and competencies) that may determine successful business sustainability in terms of the environment for SMEs?" In addition to leaders' attributes, three different sustainability performance measurement dimensions emerged: financial, internal sustainability process dimension, and value dimension. Two of these dimensions match with two of the conventional BSC aspects (financial and internal process dimensions) mentioned in the literature review chapter.

CHAPTER 7

Summary and Recommendation

Summary

Researchers have studied leaders' attributes for many years. However, there is little research focused on the attributes for the sustainability leader, especially in the eastern culture. This study empirically examined the role of personality trait and attributes. It is a first approach to conceptualize and create a model for sustainability leaders in Arabic and eastern cultures based around skills. The model describes leadership in terms of leaders' skills and attributes which can help to drive their firms to the sustainability business era. This model suggests that certain types of characteristics, qualities, and skills are especially important for leaders to succeed in adopting the sustainability activities in their firms.

Very few or no studies have addressed sustainability leader attributes in Egypt and the Middle East. This research, thus, attempts to discover and address attributes in a new context and under different conditions. The qualitative grounded theory is selected to develop in-depth understanding around the sustainability leader attributes about which little has been written. The author seeks to generate theory directly from data collected without relying on the guidance of theory-generated hypotheses as advocated in the traditional positivist scientific research methodology. Consequently the author suggested that some of the sustainability leader attributes which are mentioned earlier may be manifested while others that are not mentioned have been raised as a result of this study. Grounded theory had been used to generate theory therefore creating an inventory of assumptions and hypotheses that can positively affect the mindset of managers and leaders in SMEs.

The conceptual model which emerged from this study was developed from in-depth interviews with sustainability leaders, sustainable firms' observation, and extensive review of existing research in both academic and practical contexts.

Findings that emerged from the study illustrated that systemic thinking, individual consideration, authoritarian, expertise and knowledge, persistence, charismatic, democratic, and personality traits are antecedents to sustainable leader attributes. In addition there are three different sustainability performance measurement dimensions: financial, internal sustainability process dimension and value dimension emerged.

Findings from this study might apply just as well to different countries in the Middle Eastern region, though it would be advised to conduct similar studies in these countries. Research about leadership styles has shown that there are specific behaviors which prove that styles may differ from culture to culture. "The members of the same culture are more likely to interpret and evaluate situational events in a similar way than those from different cultures" (Shahin and Wright 2004, p. 501).

It may be convenient to apply leadership theories of North American origin to a region but not to another (Shahin and Wright 2004). The authors suggest that generally, different leadership theories are not applied with the same outcome in different regions or cultures. The important role of local or regional leaders cannot be ignored when influencing the environmental and social process of moving from discussion to action and identifying innovative responses to their local context concerning sustainability problem (Keys et al. 2010). According to Keys et al. (2010), turning to the local or regional leaders may help identify innovative ideas to solve the sustainability problems for their local context. Thus, this research investigated the sustainability leader model in a Middle Eastern country, in this case Egypt, by means of an in-depth study of the attributes of sustainability leaders in a Middle Eastern emerging nation, whose culture differs significantly from that of western countries, working inductively by building logical explanations of phenomena through observing in-depth social practices and events in organizations concerned about local sustainability leaders.

Recommendation for Future Research

A possible limitation of this study was the lack of participation of leaders in nonprofit organizations during data collection. All in-depth interviews were held with the most senior managers. Middle management was not interviewed.

The author supposes that the study is of significance and will encourage future research into validating the study in nonprofit organizations and in other countries with different cultures. Opportunities also exist for future research to test the key individual's sustainability leader attributes, which emerged from this research, across quantitative scales in other cultures to measure responses on complex sustainability issues.

Bibliography

Administration, U.I. 2014. "Country Analysis Brief: Egypt." http://eia.gov/countries/country-data.cfm?fips=EG

Andreas, F., E.S. Cooperman, B. Gifford, and G. Russell, eds. 2011. *A Simple Path to Sustainability: Green Business Strategies for Small and Medium-Sized Businesses*. Santa Barbara, CA: ABC-Clio.

Anderson, T.L., L.E. Huggins, and M. Friedman. 2003. "The Property Rights Path to Sustainable Development." *Free to Choose* 57.

Aryee, S., Z.X. Chen, L. Sun, and Y.A. Debrah. 2007. "Antecedents and Outcomes of Abusive Supervision: Test of a Trickle-down Model." *The Journal of Applied Psychology* 92, no. 1, 191–201. https://doi.org/10.1037/0021-9010.92.1.191.

Aubert, M.F., R. Cortopassi, G. Nachtergael, P. Détienne, and A.S. Le Hô. 2008. *Portraits funéraires de l'Egypte romaine*.

Avolio, B.J., and B.M. Bass. 1995. "Individual Consideration Viewed at Multiple Levels of Analysis: A Multi-Level Framework for Examining the Diffusion of Transformational Leadership." *The Leadership Quarterly* 6, no. 2, pp. 199–218.

Backman, K., and H.A. Kyngäs. 1999. "Challenges of the Grounded Theory Approach to a Novice Researcher." *Nursing & Health Sciences* 1, pp. 147–53.

Badaracco Jr, J.L. 2001. "We Don't Need Another Hero." *Harvard Business Review* 79, no. 8, pp. 120–26.

Bakel, J.C., D.A. Loorbach, and G.M. Whiteman. 2007. *Business Strategies for Transitions Towards Sustainable Systems* (No. ERS-2007-094-ORG). ERIM Report Series Research in Management.

Bansal, P. 2005. "Evolving Sustainably: A Longitudinal Study of Corporate Sustainable Development." *Strat. Mgmt. J* 26.

Bass, B.M., and R.M Stogdill. 1990. *Bass & Stogdill's Handbook of Leadership: Theory, Research, and Managerial Applications*. Simon and Schuster.

Bell, J., and J. Stellingwerf. 2012. *Sustainable Entrepreneurship: The Motivations and Challenges of Sustainable Entrepreneurs in the Renewable Energy Industry*. (Unpublished master's thesis). Jönköping. Sweden.

Blewitt, J. 2008. *Understanding Sustainable Development*. London: Earthscan.

BSD Global. 2002. "Business and Sustainable Development." https://iisd.org/business/ (accessed April 15, 2016).

Blodgett, J.G., A. Bakir, and G.M. Rose. 2008. "A Test of the Validity of Hofstede's Cultural Framework." *Journal of Consumer Marketing* 25, pp. 339–49.

Bogumil, J., and S. Immerfall. 1985. *Wahrnehmungsweisen Empirischer Sozial-Forschung*. Frankfurt/New York: Campus.

Bonn, I. 2001. *Developing Strategic Thinking as a Core Competency, Manage- Ment Decision* 39, no. 1, pp. 63–70.

Bonn, I. 2005. "Improving Strategic Thinking: A Multilevel Approach." *Leadership & Amp Organization Development Journal* 26, pp. 336–54.

Bolden, R. 2011. "Leadership in Organizations: A Review of Theory and Research." *International Journal of Management Reviews* 13, pp. 251–69.

Bowman, C., and V. Ambrosini. 2000. "Value Creation versus Value Capture: Towards a Coherent Definition of Value in Strategy." *British Journal of Management* 11, no. 1.

Boyatzis, R.E., D. Goleman, and H. Acquisition. 2007. *Emotional and Social Competency Inventory*. Boston, MA: Hay Group.

Brown, M.E., and L.K. Treviño. 2006. "Leadership: A Review and Future Directions." *The Leadership Quarterly* 17, pp. 595–616.

Bunning, R., and T. Berry. 2006. *Leadership*. Edinburgh Business School. Heriot- Watt University.

Cameron, K.S. 1994. "Strategies for Successful Organizational Downsizing." *Hu- Man Resource Management* 33, pp. 189–211.

Caraiani, C., C.I. Lungu, C. Dascălu, M.V. Cimpoeru, and M. Dinu. 2012. "Social and Environmental Performance Indicators: Dimensions of Integrated Reporting and Benefits for Responsible Management and Sustainability." *African Journal of Business Management* 6, pp. 4990–97.

Carmeli, A. 2003. "The Relationship between Emotional Intelligence and Work Attitudes, Behavior and Outcomes: An Examination among Senior Managers." *Journal of Managerial Psychology* 18, pp. 788–813.

Chatrchyan, S., V. Khachatryan, A.M. Sirunyan, A. Tumasyan, W. Adam, E. Agui- lo, and M. Friedl. 2012. "Observation of a New Boson at a Mass of 125 GeV with the CMS Experiment at the LHC." *Physics Letters B* 716, pp. 30–61.

Charmaz, K. 2014. *Constructing Grounded Theory*. London: Sage.

Choi, S. 2007. "Democratic Leadership: The Lessons of Exemplary Models for Democratic Governance." *International Journal of Leadership Studies* 2, pp. 243–62.

Choi, Y., and R.R. Mai-Dalton. 1999. "The Model of Followers' Responses to Self- Sacrificial Leadership: An Empirical Test." *The Leadership Quarterly* 10, pp. 397–421.

Chukwuma, C. 1995. "Environmental, Developmental and Health Perspectives in Egypt." *Environmental Management and Health* 6, pp. 29–37.

Crawford, D., and T. Scaletta. 2006. "The Balanced Scorecard and Corporate Social Responsibility: Aligning Values for Profit." *Inside FMIJ* 17, p. 39.

Dearborn, K. 2002. "Studies in Emotional Intelligence Redefine Our Approach to Leadership Development." *Public Personnel Management* 31, pp. 523–30.

De Leeuw, L., K. Bubna-Litic, and R. Genoff. 2000. "Implementing the Green Advantage in Small and Medium Sized Enterprises." *Proceedings of the 9th Greening of Industry Conference*. Bangkok: Environmental Research Institute, Chulalongkorn University.

DeSantis, T. Z., P. Hugenholtz, N. Larsen, M. Rojas, E.L. Brodie, K. Keller, T. Huber, D. Dalevi, P. Hu, and G.L. Andersen. 2006. "Greengenes, a Chimera-Checked 16S RRNA Gene Database and Workbench Compatible with ARB." *Applied and Environmental Microbiology* 72, pp. 5069–72.

Dey, I. 2003. *Qualitative Data Analysis: A User Friendly Guide for Social Scientists*. London: Routledge.

Duncan, W.J. 1978. *Organizational Behaviour*. Boston, MA: Houghton Mifflin.

Dutra, A., P. Everaert, S. Fust, and J. Millen. 2011. "Leadership Styles That Drive Sustainability." *Paper Presented at the World Business Council for Sustain- Able Development, US Midwest Regional Meeting*. Columbus, OH.

Dvir, T., D. Eden, B.J. Avolio, and B Shamir. 2002. "Impact of Transformational Leadership on Follower Development and Performance: A Field Experiment." *Academy of Management Journal* 45, pp. 735–44.

Eagly, A.H., M.C. Johannesen-Schmidt, and M.L Van Engen. 2003. *Transformational, Transactional, and Laissez-Faire Leadership Styles: A Meta-Analysis Comparing Women and Men*.

Eccles, R.G., and M.P. Krzus. 2010. *One Report: Integrated Reporting for a Sus-Tainable Strategy*. New York, NJ: Wiley.

ElKhouly, S.E., and R. Marwan. 2016. "Defining the Organizational Culture That Drives Strategic Innovation in Micro, Small and Medium Enterprises in Egypt." *In Competition Forum*, Vol 14, p. 190. American Society for Competitiveness.

Elkington, J. 1998. *Cannibals with Forks (p.5)*. Gabriola Island, BC: New Society Publishers.

Elkington, J. 1997. *Cannibals with Forks. The Triple Bottom Line of 21st Century*. Capstone.

El-Kot, G., and M. Leat. 2005. "Investigating Team Work in the Egyptian Context." *Personnel Review* 34, pp. 246–61.

Elsaid, E., and A.M Elsaid. 2012. "Culture and Leadership: Comparing Egypt to the GLOBE Study of 62 Societies." *Business and Management Research* 1.

Enquist, B., Johnson, M., & Skålén, P. 2006. "Adoption of Corporate Social Responsibility–Incorporating a Stakeholder Perspective." *Qualitative Research in Accounting & Management* 3, pp. 188–207.

Environmental and Energy Study Institution. 2014. "Fossil Fuels." http://eesi.org/topics/fossil-fuels/description.

Epstein, M.J., and M.J. Roy. 2001. "Sustainability in Action: Identifying and Measuring the Key Performance Drivers." *Long Range Planning* 34, pp. 585–604.

Ethiraj, S.K., P. Kale, M.S. Krishnan, and J.V. Singh. 2005. "Where Do Capabilities Come from and How Do They Matter? A Study in the Software Services Industry." *Strategic Management Journal* 26, pp. 25–45.

Fiksel, J., J. McDaniel, and C. Mendenhall. 1999. "Measuring Progress towards Sustainability Principles, Process, and Best Practices." *In Greening of Industry Network Conference Best Practice Proceedings*, http://economics.com/images/Sustainability%20Measurement%20GIN.pdf (accessed June 2012).

Fitzsimons, D., K.T. James, and D. Denyer. 2011. "Alternative Approaches for Studying Shared and Distributed Leadership." *International Journal of Management Reviews* 13, pp. 313–28.

Friedman, A.L., S. Miles, and C. Adams. 2000. "Small and Medium-Sized Enterprises and the Environment: Evaluation of a Specific Initiative Aimed at All Small and Medium-Sized Enterprises." *Journal of Small Business and Enterprise Development* 7, pp. 325–42.

Gartner, W.B., and K.G Shaver. 2012. "Nascent Entrepreneurship Panel Studies: Progress and Challenges." *Small Business Economics* 39, pp. 659–65.

Gastil, J. 1994. "A Definition and Illustration of Democratic Leadership." *Human Relations* 47, pp. 953–75.

Ghaem, A. 2013. *The Relationship between Transformational Leadership and Organizational Sustainability.* (Unpublished Master's thesis). Maastricht School of Management, the Netherlands.

Ghobadian, A., H. Viney, J. Liu, and P. James. 1998. "Extending Linear Approaches to Mapping Corporate Environmental Behaviour." *Business Strategy and the Environment* 7, pp. 13–23.

Grant, D. 2007. "Business Histories and Biographies: An Introduction." *Business Information Review* 4, pp. 29–32.

Glaser, B.G. 2008. "Conceptualization: On Theory and Theorizing Using Grounded Theory." *International Journal of Qualitative Methods* 1, pp. 23–38.

Glaser, B.G. 1978. *Theoretical Sensitivity: Advances in the Methodology of Grounded Theory*, Vol. 2. Mill Valley, CA: Sociology Press.

Glaser, B., and A. Strauss. 1967. *The Discovery of Grounded Theory.* London, England: Weidenfield & Nicolson.

Godfrey, M., and A. Manikas. 2012. "Integrating Triple Bottom Line Sustainability Concepts into a Supplier Selection Exercise." *Business Education & Accreditation* 4, pp. 1–12.

Golafshani, N. 2003. "Understanding Reliability and Validity in Qualitative Research." *The Qualitative Report* 8, pp. 597–607.

Graetz, F. 2002. "Strategic Thinking versus Strategic Planning: Towards under-Standing the Complementarities." *Management Decision* 40, pp. 456–62.

Graham, R., and S Bertels. 2008. "Achieving Sustainable Value: Sustainability Portfolio Assessment." *Greener Management International* 54.

Gunia, B.C., N. Sivanathan, and A.D. Galinsky. 2009. "Vicarious Entrapment: Your Sunk Costs, My Escalation of Commitment." *Journal of Experimental Social Psychology* 45, pp. 1238–44.

Hanford, P. 1995. "Developing Director and Executive Competencies in Strategic Thinking." In B. Garratt, ed. *Developing Strategic Thought: Reinventing the Art of Direction-Giving,* 157–86. London: McGraw-Hill.

Hammersley, M. 1992. *What's Wrong with Ethnography? Methodological Explorations.* Oxford: Psychology Press.

Hardman, J. 2010. "Regenerative Leadership: A Model for Transforming People and Organizations for Sustainability in Business, Education, and Community." *Integral Leadership Review* 10, pp. 1–17.

Hart, S. 1995. "A Natural-Resource-Based View of the Firm." *The Academy Of Management Review* 20.

Harry, J. 2015. "Business and Sustainable Development." Vol 6, http://dx.-doi.org/10.9774/gleaf.8757.2015.ju.00007

Hazy, J.K., J. Goldstein, and B.B. Lichtenstein. eds. 2007. *Complex Systems Leadership Theory: New Perspectives from Complexity Science on Social and Organizational Effectiveness.* ISCE Pub.

Henman, L.D. 2011. "Leadership: Theories and Controversies." http://henmanperformancegroup.com/articles/Leadership-Theories.pdf

Hillary, R., ed. 2000. *Small and Medium-Sized Enterprises and the Environment: Business Imperatives.* London, England: Greenleaf Publishing.

Hillman, A.J., G.D. Keim. 2001. "Shareholder Value, Stakeholder Management, and Social Issues: What's the Bottom Line?" *Strategic Management Journal* 22.

Hind, P., A. Wilson, and G. Lenssen. 2009. "Developing Leaders for Sustainable Business." *Corporate Governance* 9, pp. 7–20.

Hofstede, G. 1980. *Culture's Consequences: International Differences in Work Related Values.* Beverly Hills, CA: Sage Publications.

Hofstede, G. 1993. "Cultural Constraints in Management Theories." *The Academy of Management Executive* 7, pp. 81–94.

Hofstede, G. (n.d.). "Egypt in Comparison with United States and United Kingdom." http://geert-hofstede.com/egypt.html (accessed December 10, 2014).

Hogan, R.T., G.J. Curphy, and J. Hogan. 1994. "What We Know About Leadership: Effectiveness and Personality." *American Psychologist* 49, pp. 493–504.

Holland, D.V., and D.A. Shepherd. 2013. "Deciding to Persist: Adversity, Values, and Entrepreneurs' Decision Policies." *Entrepreneurship Theory and Practice* 37, no. 2, pp. 331–58.

Howarth, R., and J. Fredericks. 2012. "Sustainable SME Practice: A Reflection on Supply-Chain Environmental Management Intervention." *Management of Environmental Quality: An International Journal* 23, pp. 673–85.

Howell, J.M., and B. Shamir. 2005. "The Role of Followers in the Charismatic Leadership Process: Relationships and their Consequences." *Academy of Management Review* 30, pp. 96–112.

Idrees, I., Vasconcelos, A.C., and A.M. Cox. March, 2011. "The Use of Grounded Theory in PhD Research in Knowledge Management: A Model Four-Stage Research Design." In *Aslib Proceedings*, Vol. 63, 188–203. Emerald Group.

International Models for Sustainable Development. 2010. "Business Models for Sustainable Development." http://iied.org/busi- ness-models-for-sustainable-development (accessed April 15, 2016).

Judge, T.A., C.J. Thoresen, J.E. Bono, and G.K. Patton. 2001. "The Job Satisfaction–Job Performance Relationship: A Qualitative and Quantitative Review." *Psychological Bulletin* 127, p. 376.

Kara, A., and C.L. Arnold. 2010. "Individually Considerate Transformational Leadership Behavior and Self Sacrifice." *Leadership & Organization Development Journal* 31, pp. 670–86.

Kempster, S., and K.W. Parry. 2011. "Grounded Theory and Leadership Research: A Critical Realist Perspective." *The Leadership Quarterly* 22, no. 1, pp. 106–20.

Keys, N., D.C. Thomsen, and T.F. Smith. 2010. "Opinion Leaders and Complex Sustainability Issues." *Management of Environmental Quality: An International Journal* 21, pp. 187–97.

Kolb, S.M. 2012. "Grounded Theory and the Constant Comparative Method: Valid Research Strategies for Educators." *Journal of Emerging Trends in Educational Research and Policy Studies* 3, pp. 83–86.

Kotter, J.P. 2013. "Management Is (Still) Not Leadership." *Harvard Business Review Blog.* January 9.

Kotter, J.P. 1998. "Winning at Change." *Leader to Leader* 10, pp. 27–33.

Lakshman, C. 2008. "Attributional Theory of Leadership: A Model of Functional Attributions and Behaviors." *Leadership & Organization Development Journal* 29, pp. 317–19.

Lacy, P., and R. Hayward. 2011. "A New Era of Sustainability in Emerging Markets? Insights from a Global CEO Study by the United Nations Global Compact and Accenture." *Corporate Governance* 11, pp. 348–357.

Leadership Theories. (n.d.). http://leadership-central.com/leadership-theories. html#axzz3M6iMmTz4 (accessed December 17, 2014).

LeCompte, M.D., and J.P. Goetz. 1982. "Problems of Reliability and Validity in Ethnographic Research." *Review of Educational Research* 52, pp. 31–60.

Liao, J., and W.B. Gartner. 2006. "The Effects of Pre-Venture Plan Timing and Perceived Environmental Uncertainty on the Persistence of Emerging Firms." *Small Business Economics* 27, pp. 23–40.

Liedtka, J.M. 1998. "Strategic Thinking: Can It Be Taught?" *Long Range Planning* 31, pp. 120–29.

Lincoln, Y.S., and E.G. Guba. 1985. *Naturalistic Inquiry.* Beverly Hills, CA: Sage.

Linnenluecke, M., and A. Griffiths. 2010. "Beyond Adaptation: Resilience for Business in Light of Climate Change and Weather Extremes." *Business & Society* 49, pp. 477–511.

Locke, K. 2001. *Grounded Theory in Management Research.* Sage.

Lombard, L., K. April, and K. Peters. 2012. "Sustainability and Authentic Leadership: Stumbling Blocks and Enablers." *Crown Research in Education* 2, pp. 74–84.

Loorbach, D., J.C. Bakel, G. Whiteman, and J. Rotmans. 2010. "Business Strategies for Transitions towards Sustainable Systems." *Business Strategy and the Environment* 19, pp. 133–46.

Lorenzoni, I., A. Jordan, M. Hulme, R. Kerry Turner, and T. O'Riordan. 2000. "A Co-Evolutionary Approach to Climate Change Impact Assessment: Part I. Integrating Socio-Economic and Climate Change Scenarios." *Global Environmental Change* 10, pp. 57–68.

Loewe, M., I. Al-Ayouty, A. Altpeter, L. Borbein, M. Chantelauze, M. Kern, and M. Reda. 2013. "Which Factors Determine the Upgrading of Small and Medium- Sized Enterprises (SMEs)? The Case of Egypt." *The Case of Egypt. The German Development Institute.*

Lynam, A. 2012. "Navigating a Geography of Sustainability Worldviews: A Developmental Map." *Journal of Sustainability Education* 3, pp. 1–14.

Marton, F., A.B. Tsui, P.P. Chik, P.Y. Ko, and M.L. Lo. 2004. *Classroom Discourse and the Space of Learning.* Routledge.

McEwen, C.A., and J.D. Schmidt. 2007. "Leadership and the Corporate Sustainability Challenge: Mindsets in Action."

McMullen, J.S., and D.A. Shepherd. 2006. "Entrepreneurial Action and the Role of Uncertainty in the Theory of the Entrepreneur." *Academy of Management Review* 31, pp. 132–52.

McGregor, D. 1960. *The Human Side of Enterprise.* New York: McGraw-Hill, Inc.

Menon, A., and A. Menon. 1997. "Enviropreneurial Marketing Strategy: The Emergence of Corporate Environmentalism as Market Strategy." *The Journal of Marketing*, pp. 51–67.

Metcalf, L., and S. Benn. 2013. "Leadership for Sustainability: An Evolution of Leadership Ability." *Journal of Business Ethics* 112, pp. 369–84.

Merz, E.L., and S.C. Roesch. 2011. "Modeling Trait and State Variation Using Multi- Level Factor Analysis with PANAS Daily Diary Data." *Journal of Research in Personality* 45, no. 1, pp. 2–9.

Minkov, M., and G. Hofstede. 2011. "The Evolution of Hofstede's Doctrine." *Cross Cultural Management: An International Journal* 18, pp. 10–20.

Mintzberg, H. 1994a. *The Rise and Fall of Strategic Planning*. Free Press and Prentice Hall International, Hertfordshire.

Mintzberg, H. 1994b. "The Fall and Rise of Strategic Planning." *Harvard Business Review*, pp. 107–14.

Mintzberg, H., B. Ahlstrand, and J. Lampel. 1998a. *Strategy Safari*. Prentice Hall, Hertfordshire.

Mintzberg, H., J.B. Quinn, and S. Ghoshal. 1998b. *The Strategy Process*. Revised European. Prentice Hall, Hertfordshire.

Miles, M.B., and A.M. Huberman. 1994. *Qualitative Data Analysis: An Expanded Sourcebook*. London: Sage.

Millar, C.C.J.M., and M. Gitsham. 2013. "The Role of Management Development in Achieving a Culture Change towards Sustainability in the Organisation." *Journal of Management Development* 32.

Mirvis, P.H., and J. Manga. 2010. "Integrating Corporate Citizenship: Leading from the Middle." In *Global Challenges in Responsible Business*, pp. 78–106.

Morsing, M., and D. Oswald. 2009. "Sustainable Leadership: Management Control Systems and Organizational Culture in Novo Nordisk A/S." *Corporate Governance* 9, pp. 83–99.

Morrison, A., J. Breen, and S. Ali. 2003. "Small Business Growth: Intention, Ability, and Opportunity." *Journal of Small Business Management* 41, pp. 417–25.

Mumford, M.D., S.J. Zaccaro, F.D. Harding, T.O. Jacobs, and E.A. Fleishman. 2000. "Leadership Skills for a Changing World: Solving Complex Social Problems." *The Leadership Quarterly* 11, pp. 11–35.

Muralidaran, S. 2013. "Pollution in Egypt: Global Consequences to Poor Environmental Practices. The Triple Helix Online; a Global Forum of Science in Society." http://triplehelixblog.com/2013/05/pollution-in-egypt-global-consequences-to-poor-environmental-practices/

Nonaka, I. 1991. *Models of Knowledge Management in the West and Japan*.

Nonaka, I., and H. Takeuchi. 1995. *The Knowledge Creation Company: How Japanese Companies Create the Dynamics of Innovation*.

Nuntamanop, P., I. Kauranen, and I. Barbara. 2013. "A New Model of Strategic Thinking Competency." *Journal of Strategy and Management* 6, pp. 242–64.

Nyström, M.E., E. Höög, R. Garvare, L. Weinehall, and A. Ivarsson. 2013. "Change and Learning Strategies in Large Scale Change Programs: Describing the Variation of Strategies Used in a Health Promotion Program." *Journal of Organizational Change Management* 26, pp. 1020–44.

O'Reilly, C.A., and J. Chatman. 1986. "Organizational Commitment and Psychological Attachment: The Effects of Compliance, Identification, and Internalization on Prosocial Behavior." *Journal of Applied Psychology* 71, p. 492.

Parnell, J.A., and T. Hatem. 1999. "Cultural Antecedents of Behavioural Differences between American and Egyptian Managers." *Journal of Management Studies* 36, pp. 399–418.

Pauleen, D.J., B. Corbitt, and P. Yoong. 2007. "Discovering and Articulating What Is Not yet Known: Using Action Learning and Grounded Theory as a Knowledge Management Strategy." *The Learning Organization* 14, pp. 222–40.

Paulsen, N., D. Maldonado, J.C. Victor, and A. Oluremi. 2009. "Charismatic Leadership, Change and Innovation in an R&D Organization." *Journal of Organizational Change Management* 22, pp. 511–23.

Pearce, C.L., C.C. Manz, and S. Akanno. 2013. "Searching for the Holy Grail of Management Development and Sustainability: Is Shared Leadership Development the Answer?" *Journal of Management Development* 32, pp. 247–57.

Peräkylä, A. 2011. "Validity in Research on Naturally Occurring Social Interaction." *Qualitative Research*. pp. 365–82.

Perrini, F., A. Russo, A. Tencati, and C. Perry. 2007. "CSR Strategies of SMEs and Large Firms.,Processes of a Case Study Methodology for Postgraduate Research in Marketing." *Evidence from Italy. Journal of Business Ethics,,European Journal of Marketing* 74, pp. 285–300, 785–802.

Petrini, M., and M. Pozzebon. 2010. "Integrating Sustainability into Business Prac- Tices: Learning from Brazilian Firms." *BAR-Brazilian Administration Review* 7, pp. 362–78.

Pickard, A.J. 2007. *Research Methods in Information*. London: Facet Publishing.

Pierro, A., L. Cicero, M. Bonaiuto, D. Knippenberg, and A.W. Kruglanski. 2005. "Leader Group Prototypicality and Leadership Effectiveness: The Moderating Role of Need for Cognitive Closure." *The Leadership Quarterly* 16, pp. 503–16.

Porter, M.E. 1985, *Competitive Advantage—Creating and Sustaining Superior Performance*. The Free Press, Hertfordshire.

Porter, M.E. May 23, 1987. "Corporate Strategy—The State of Strategic Thinking." *The Economist*, pp. 19–22.

Porter, M.E. November-December, 1996. "What Is Strategy?" *Harvard Business Review*, pp. 61–78.

Prussia, G.E., J.S. Anderson, and C.C. Manz. 1998. "Self-Leadership and Performance Outcomes: The Mediating Influence of Self-Efficacy." *Journal of Organizational Behavior* 19, pp. 523–38.

Quinn, L., and J. Baltes. 2007. *Leadership and the Triple Bottom Line*. Greensboro, NC: Center for Creative Leadership.

Rafferty, A.E., and M.A. Griffin. 2006. "Perceptions of Organizational Change: A Stress and Coping Perspective." *The Journal of Applied Psychology* 91, pp. 1154–62.

Rebitzer, G., T. Ekvall, R. Frischknecht, D. Hunkeler, G. Norris, T. Rydberg, W.P. Schmidt, S. Suh, B.P. Weidema, and D.W. Pennington. 2004. "Life Cycle Assessment Part 1: Framework, Goal and Scope Definition, Inventory Analysis, and Applications." *Environment International* 30, pp. 701–20.

Remler, D.K., and G.G. Van Ryzin. 2014. *Research Methods in Practice: Strategies for Description and Causation*. London: Sage. http://balancedscorecard. org/Portals/0/PDF/LinkingSustain-abilitytoCorporateStrategyUsingthe BalancedScorecard. pdf

Robert, K., T. Parris, and A. Leiserowitz. 2005. "What is Sustainable Development? Goals, Indicators, Values, and Practice." *Environment: Science and Policy for Sustainable Development* 47, pp. 8–21.

Rohm, H., and D. Montgomery. 2011. *Link Sustainability to Corporate Strategy Using the Balanced Scorecard*.

Rondinelli, D., and M. Berry. 2000. "Environmental Citizenship in Multinational Corporations: Social Responsibility and Sustainable Development." *European Management Journal* 18.

Rooke, D., and W.R. Torbert. 2005. "7 Transformations of Leadership." *Harvard Business Review* 83, pp. 66–76, 133.

Ruf, B.M., K. Muralidhar, R.M. Brown, J.J. Janney, and K. Paul. 2001. "An Empirical Investigation of the Relationship between Change in Corporate Social Performance and Financial Performance: A Stakeholder Theory Perspective." *Journal of Business Ethics* 32, pp. 143–56.

Sarantakos, S. 1994. *Social Research*. London: Sage.

Saunders, M., P. Lewis, and A. Thornhill. 2011. *Research Methods for Business Students*. Pearson Education India.

Schaltegger, S., and M. Wagner. 2006. "Integrative Management of Sustainability Performance, Measurement and Reporting." *International Journal of Accounting, Auditing and Performance Evaluation* 3, pp. 1–19.

Schein, E.H. 2010. *Organizational Culture and Leadership*, Vol. 2. New York, NY: Wiley.

Schuh, S.C., X.A. Zhang, and P. Tian. 2013. "For the Good or the Bad? Interactive Effects of Transformational Leadership with Moral and Authoritarian Leadership Behaviors." *Journal of Business Ethics* 116, pp. 629–40.

Schwalb, P.G. 2011. *Sustainability Leader Competencies: A Grounded Theory Study.* Lincoln, US: University of Nebraska.

Shamir, B., R.J. House, and M.B. Arthur. 1993. "The Motivational Effects of Charismatic Leadership: A Self-Concept Based Theory." *Organization Science* 4, pp. 577–94.

Sebhatu, S.P. 2009. *Sustainability Performance Measurement for Sustainable Organizations: Beyond Compliance and Reporting.* Sweden: Karlstad University.

Shahin, A.I., and P.L. Wright. 2004. "Leadership in the Context of Culture: An Egyptian Perspective." *Leadership & Organization Development Journal* 25, pp. 499–511.

Shang, H., M.M. Frank, E.P. Gusev, J.O. Chu, S.W. Bedell, K.W. Guarini, and M. Ieong. 2006. "Germanium Channel MOSFETs: Opportunities and Challenges." *IBM Journal of Research and Development* 50, pp. 377–86.

Somech, A. 2006. "The Effects of Leadership Style and Team Process on Perfor-Mance and Innovation in Functionally Heterogeneous Teams." *Journal of Management* 32, pp. 132–57.

Soyka, P.A. 2012. *Creating a Sustainable Organization: Approaches for Enhancing Corporate Value through Sustainability.* London, England: FT.

Starik, M. 1995. "Should Trees Have Managerial Standing? Toward Stakeholder Status for Non-Human Nature." *Journal of Business* 14.

Stake, R.E. 1998. *Teacher Evaluation.* University of Illinois, Urbana-Champaign.

Steven, R. 2014. "Knowledge Influencers: Leaders Influencing Knowledge Cre- Ation and Mobilization." *Journal of Educational Administration* 52, pp. 332–57.

Stoughton, A.M., and J. Ludema. 2012. "The Driving Forces of Sustainability." *Journal of Organizational Change Management* 25, pp. 501–17.

Strauss, A., and Corbin. 1998. *Basics of Qualitative Research. Techniques and Procedures for Developing Grounded Theory.* Thousand Oaks.

Strauss, A.L. 1987. *Qualitative Analysis for Social Scientists.* Cambridge, UK: Cambridge University Press.

State Information Service in Egypt (n.d.) "Environment." http://sis.gov.eg/En/Templates/Articles/tmpArticles.aspx?CatID=801#.VIyfB- vlSmw1

Stern, N. 2007. *The Economics of Climate Change: The Stern Review.* Cambridge, UK: Cambridge University Press.

Substitutes for Leadership Theory. (n.d.). http://en.wikipedia.org/wiki/Substitutes_for_Leadership_Theory

Sustainability Leadership Institute. October, 2014. *Sustainability Leaders' Definition.* http://sustainabilityleadershipinstitute.org/leadership.php

Sustainable Development Commission. (n.d.). "What's Sustainable Developement." http://sd-commission.org.uk/pages/what-is-sustainable-development.html

Sveiby, K.E. 2001. "Knowledge-Based Theory of the Firm." *Journal of Intellectual Capital* 2, pp. 344–58.

Tang, K., D.A. Robinson, and M. Harvey. 2011. "Sustainability Managers or Rogue Mid-Managers? A Typology of Corporate Sustainability Managers." *Management Decision* 49, pp. 1371–94.

Tavakoli, I., and J. Lawton. 2005. "Strategic Thinking and Knowledge Management." *Handbook of Business Strategy* 6, pp. 155–60.

Taylor, A. 2011. "The Role of Leadership for Environment and Sustainability." Perspectives on Environment and Sustainability. http://water-centre.org/

Taylor, A. 2009. "Responding to the Challenge of Climate Change: Using the Lever of Leadership." In *Managing Waste in a Changing Climate Conference*, 4–6. Launceston, Tasmania.

Tilley, F. 1999. "The Gap between the Environmental Attitudes and the Environmental Behaviour of Small Firms." *Business Strategy and the Environment* 8, pp. 238–48.

Tovstiga, G. 2010. *Strategy in Practice: A Practitioner's Guide to Strategic Thinking*. Chichester: John Wiley.

Tregoe, B.B., and J.W. Zimmerman. 1980. *Top Management Strategy*. New York, NY: Simon & Schuster.

Vavra, J., M. Bednarikova, and Z. Ehlova. 2012. "Assessment of Sustainability As- Pects in a Company." *The 7th International Scientific Conference Business and Management 2012*. Lithuania: Vilnius Gedimina Technical University.

Visser, W., and P. Courtice. 2011. "Leadership: Linking Theory and Practice." *Social Science Research Network*, http://ssrn.com/abstract=1947221

Waldman, D.A., and D. Siegel. 2008. "Defining the Socially Responsible Leader." *The Leadership Quarterly* 19, pp. 117–31.

Watson, S. 2007. "Developing Shared Leadership: A Hands-off Approach." *Distributed and Shared Leadership Edited by Professor David Collinson* 8, pp. 27–42.

Western, S. 2010. "Eco-Leadership, towards the Development of a New Paradigm." *Leadership for Environmental Sustainability*, pp. 36–54.

William, M., and D.W. Williams. 2017. "Venture Creation Persistence: Overcoming Stage-Gate Issues." *International Journal of Entrepreneurial Behavior & Research*.

Wisner, P.S., M.J. Epstein, and R.P. Bagozzi. 2006. "Organizational Antecedents and Consequences of Environmental Performance." *Advances in Environmental Accounting & Management* 3, pp. 143–67.

Wheelen, T.L., and J.D. Hunger. 2011. *Concepts in Strategic Management and Business Policy: Toward Global Sustainability*. 13th. New Jersey, NY: Pearson.

White, R.K., and R. Lippitt. 1960. *Autocracy and Democracy: An Experimental Inquiry*. New York, NY: Harper.

Whittaker, R., R. Borland, C. Bullen, R.B. Lin, H. McRobbie, and A. Rodgers. 2009. "Mobile Phone-Based Interventions for Smoking Cessation." *Cochrane Database Syst Rev* 4.

Wood, D.J. 1991. "Corporate Social Performance Revisited." *Academy of Management Review* 16.

York-Barr, J., and K. Duke. 2004. "What Do We Know about Teacher Leadership? Findings from Two Decades of Scholarship." *Review of Educational Research* 74, pp. 255–316.

Yu, J., and J.N.B. Bell. 2007. "Building a Sustainable Business in China's Small and Medium-Sized Enterprises (SMEs)." *Journal of Environmental Assessment Policy and Management* 9, pp. 19–43.

Yukl, G. 1999. "An Evaluation of Conceptual Weaknesses in Transformational and Charismatic Leadership Theories." *The Leadership Quarterly* 10, pp. 285–305.

Zaccaro, S.J., C. Kemp, and P. Bader. 2004. "Leader Traits and Attributes." *The Nature of Leadership* 101, p. 124.

Zabriskie, N. B., and A. B Huellmantel. 1991. "Developing Strategic Thinking in Senior Management." *Long Range Planning* 24, pp. 25–32.

Zubir, A.F.M., and N.F. Habidin. 2012. "The Development of Sustainable Manufacturing Practices and Sustainable Performance in Malaysian Automotive Industry." *Journal of Economics and Sustainable Development* 3, pp. 130–38.

About the Author

Amr Sukkar is a management adjunct professor at LIGS University (Hawaii, USA), business economist expert at European Union, manages/directs a leading medical company, teaches Management for MBA and DBA programs at different business schools and develops and delivers training programs (entrepreneurship, SMEs, and strategic management) at National Training Academy (NTA). He is project and strategic management consultant for several organizations. He is experienced in international and multinational corporates. He has developed a new model for sustainability leadership for Middle East SMEs in his PhD thesis; published articles focused on SMEs, leadership, governances, and sustainable development in international scientific journals; and published about leadership in a green business era and case study SMEs in Egypt. He is teaching public administration and management at several prestigious international and local universities.

Contacts
E-mails Addresses: amressamsukkar@gmail.com
YouTube: Amr Sukkar
LinkedIn: Amr Sukkar

Index

Letters 'f' or 't' after page numbers indicate figure and table, respectively.

OTHER TITLES IN THE ENVIRONMENTAL AND SOCIAL SUSTAINABILITY FOR BUSINESS ADVANTAGE COLLECTION

- *Human Resource Management for Organizational Sustainability* by Radha R. Sharma
- *Climate Change Management* by Thi Thu Huong Ha
- *Social Development Through Benevolent Business* by Kalyan Sankar Mandal
- *Developing Sustainable Supply Chains to Drive Value, Volume II* by Robert Sroufe and Steven Melnyk
- *Developing Sustainable Supply Chains to Drive Value, Volume I* by Robert P.Sroufe and Steven A. Melnyk
- *ISO 50001 Energy Management Systems* by Johannes Kals Johannes Kals
- *Feasibility Analysis for Sustainable Technologies* by Scott R. Herriott
- *The Role of Legal Compliance in Sustainable Supply Chains, Operations, and Marketing* by John Wood
- *Change Management for Sustainability* by Huong Ha
- *The Thinking Executive's Guide to Sustainability* by Kerul Kassel

Announcing the Business Expert Press Digital Library

Concise e-books business students need for classroom and research

This book can also be purchased in an e-book collection by your library as

- a one-time purchase,
- that is owned forever,
- allows for simultaneous readers,
- has no restrictions on printing, and
- can be downloaded as PDFs from within the library community.

Our digital library collections are a great solution to beat the rising cost of textbooks. E-books can be loaded into their course management systems or onto students' e-book readers.
The **Business Expert Press** digital libraries are very affordable, with no obligation to buy in future years. For more information, please visit **www.businessexpertpress.com/librarians**. To set up a trial in the United States, please email **sales@businessexpertpress.com**.